Gays in the Military

Other Books of Related Interest:

Opposing Viewpoints Series

Veterans

At Issue Series

Transgender People

Current Controversies Series

Homosexuality

"Congress shall make
no law . . . abridging
the freedom of speech,
or of the press."

First Amendment to the U.S. Constitution

The basic foundation of our democracy is the First Amendment guarantee of freedom of expression. The Opposing Viewpoints Series is dedicated to the concept of this basic freedom and the idea that it is more important to practice it than to enshrine it.

OPPOSING VIEWPOINTS® SERIES

Gays in the Military

Noah Berlatsky, Book Editor

GREENHAVEN PRESS
A part of Gale, Cengage Learning

GALE
CENGAGE Learning™

Detroit • New York • San Francisco • New Haven, Conn • Waterville, Maine • London

GALE
CENGAGE Learning™

Christine Nasso, *Publisher*
Elizabeth Des Chenes, *Managing Editor*

© 2011 Greenhaven Press, a part of Gale, Cengage Learning.

Gale and Greenhaven Press are registered trademarks used herein under license.

For more information, contact:
Greenhaven Press
27500 Drake Rd.
Farmington Hills, MI 48331-3535
Or you can visit our Internet site at gale.cengage.com

For product information and technology assistance, contact us at

Gale Customer Support, 1-800-877-4253
For permission to use material from this text or product, submit all requests online at www.cengage.com/permissions

Further permissions questions can be emailed to permissionrequest@cengage.com

Articles in Greenhaven Press anthologies are often edited for length to meet page requirements. In addition, original titles of these works are changed to clearly present the main thesis and to explicitly indicate the author's opinion. Every effort is made to ensure that Greenhaven Press accurately reflects the original intent of the authors. Every effort has been made to trace the owners of copyrighted material.

Cover image copyright © Visions of America/Joe Sohm/Digital Vision/Getty Images.

LIBRARY OF CONGRESS CATALOGING-IN-PUBLICATION DATA

Gays in the military / Noah Berlatsky, Book Editor.
   p. cm. -- (Opposing viewpoints)
   Includes bibliographical references and index.
   ISBN 978-0-7377-5221-2 (hardcover) -- ISBN 978-0-7377-5222-9 (pbk.)
   1. Gays in the military--United States. 2. Gays in the military. I. Berlatsky, Noah.
   UB418.G38G373 2011
   355.3'3086640973--dc22
                                                                2010039237

Printed in the United States of America
1 2 3 4 5 6 7 15 14 13 12 11

Contents

Chapter 3: How Is the Government Handling the Issue of Gays in the Military?

Chapter 4: How Do Other Countries Treat Gays in the Military?

Why Consider Opposing Viewpoints?

> "The only way in which a human being can make some approach to knowing the whole of a subject is by hearing what can be said about it by persons of every variety of opinion and studying all modes in which it can be looked at by every character of mind. No wise man ever acquired his wisdom in any mode but this."
>
> *John Stuart Mill*

In our media-intensive culture it is not difficult to find differing opinions. Thousands of newspapers and magazines and dozens of radio and television talk shows resound with differing points of view. The difficulty lies in deciding which opinion to agree with and which "experts" seem the most credible. The more inundated we become with differing opinions and claims, the more essential it is to hone critical reading and thinking skills to evaluate these ideas. Opposing Viewpoints books address this problem directly by presenting stimulating debates that can be used to enhance and teach these skills. The varied opinions contained in each book examine many different aspects of a single issue. While examining these conveniently edited opposing views, readers can develop critical thinking skills such as the ability to compare and contrast authors' credibility, facts, argumentation styles, use of persuasive techniques, and other stylistic tools. In short, the Opposing Viewpoints Series is an ideal way to attain the higher-level thinking and reading skills so essential in a culture of diverse and contradictory opinions.

In addition to providing a tool for critical thinking, Opposing Viewpoints books challenge readers to question their own strongly held opinions and assumptions. Most people form their opinions on the basis of upbringing, peer pressure, and personal, cultural, or professional bias. By reading carefully balanced opposing views, readers must directly confront new ideas as well as the opinions of those with whom they disagree. This is not to simplistically argue that everyone who reads opposing views will—or should—change his or her opinion. Instead, the series enhances readers' understanding of their own views by encouraging confrontation with opposing ideas. Careful examination of others' views can lead to the readers' understanding of the logical inconsistencies in their own opinions, perspective on why they hold an opinion, and the consideration of the possibility that their opinion requires further evaluation.

Evaluating Other Opinions

To ensure that this type of examination occurs, Opposing Viewpoints books present all types of opinions. Prominent spokespeople on different sides of each issue as well as well-known professionals from many disciplines challenge the reader. An additional goal of the series is to provide a forum for other, less known, or even unpopular viewpoints. The opinion of an ordinary person who has had to make the decision to cut off life support from a terminally ill relative, for example, may be just as valuable and provide just as much insight as a medical ethicist's professional opinion. The editors have two additional purposes in including these less known views. One, the editors encourage readers to respect others' opinions—even when not enhanced by professional credibility. It is only by reading or listening to and objectively evaluating others' ideas that one can determine whether they are worthy of consideration. Two, the inclusion of such viewpoints encourages the important critical thinking skill of objectively evaluating an author's credentials and bias. This evaluation will illuminate an author's reasons for taking a particular stance on an issue and will aid in readers' evaluation of the author's ideas.

It is our hope that these books will give readers a deeper understanding of the issues debated and an appreciation of the complexity of even seemingly simple issues when good and honest people disagree. This awareness is particularly important in a democratic society such as ours in which people enter into public debate to determine the common good. Those with whom one disagrees should not be regarded as enemies but rather as people whose views deserve careful examination and may shed light on one's own.

Thomas Jefferson once said that "difference of opinion leads to inquiry, and inquiry to truth." Jefferson, a broadly educated man, argued that "if a nation expects to be ignorant and free . . . it expects what never was and never will be." As individuals and as a nation, it is imperative that we consider the opinions of others and examine them with skill and discernment. The Opposing Viewpoints Series is intended to help readers achieve this goal.

David L. Bender and Bruno Leone,
Founders

Introduction

> *"Thirteen percent of all adults in the United States are veterans of the armed services. It is probable then that approximately thirteen percent of transgender people are veterans as well."*
>
> *—National Center for Transgender Equality*

"Transgender is an umbrella term for people who transition from one gender to another or who defy social expectations of how they should look, act, or identify based on their birth sex," according to an article on the Web site of the Massachusetts Transgender Political Coalition. Some transgender people may seek sex-change surgery; others may simply change the gender with which they identify.

Regulations generally prevent transgender people from serving in the military. Transgender people who have had genital surgery may be rejected during the initial physical examination for military service. If a transgender individual "has not had surgery, but identifies as transgender, the military considers this to be a mental health condition which disqualifies" the individual from military service, according to an article on the Web site of the Servicemembers Legal Defense Network. According to the same article, the military does not support surgery for currently serving transgender soldiers and may prosecute personnel who seek civilian surgery without informing the military. In addition, the military "strictly regulates uniform and grooming standards by gender," so cross-dressing in preparation for a transition, or to conform to one's preferred gender identity, may result in discipline or prosecution.

"Don't Ask, Don't Tell," or DADT, may also affect transgender service members. DADT has been the main policy regulating gay and lesbian service members. The policy prevents homosexuals from serving in the military, but also limits the military's ability to investigate soldiers' sexual orientation. Thus, service members may remain in the military as long as they hide the fact that they are gay or lesbian. DADT does not necessarily apply to transgender soldiers, since transgender soldiers do not necessarily identify as gay. However, according to the Servicemembers Legal Defense Network, transgender service members are sometimes perceived as gay or lesbian by military authorities and at times may be prosecuted under DADT.

In part to determine the extent to which DADT actually affects transgender soldiers, Karl Bryant and Kristen Schilt conducted a survey of transgender U.S. service members for the University of California–Santa Barbara's Palm Center in August 2008. This survey included responses from transgender service members "across all branches of the service." The survey found that a third of transgender service members "experienced some form of discrimination in the workplace." In the survey, 38 percent of respondents said they were suspected of being gay, and 14 percent said they were "questioned by an officer about their sexual orientation," though such questioning is not supposed to occur under the DADT policy. Bryant and Schilt concluded that "transgender service members are negatively affected by the current DADT policy, even though the policy does not directly apply to them."

As the Palm Center study shows, even though the military actively discourages the enlistment or retention of transgender service members, and despite problems caused by the DADT policy, transgender service members do exist. In fact, "some research suggests there may be a higher prevalence in the military than in society at large. That's because some young men, conflicted over their feminine feelings, enlist to try to escape them," according to a February 22, 2009, article from the McClatchy-Tribune information service posted on Military .com.

There are conflicting views about how transgender service members should be treated. Bryant and Schilt argue that the military should do more to help and accept transgender service members. DADT repeal, they say, would help in this goal, but "while repealing DADT might alleviate some of the scrutiny to which transgender service members are subject, such a policy shift would not be sufficient" to allow transgender soldiers to serve without harassment or persecution. In addition, Bryant and Schilt argue, service members should be allowed to express their chosen gender identity. They should also receive medical care for sex reassignment, whether in the military or through Veterans Administration hospitals, which currently "have a long way to go toward meeting" the needs of transgender veterans. While these steps may sound radical, they are not unprecedented. The McClatchy-Tribune article cited above noted that militaries in Canada and Britain currently not only allow transgender soldiers to serve, but "even pay for their sex-change surgeries."

On the other hand, some commentators have been strongly opposed to allowing transgender individuals in the armed forces. The Center for Military Readiness, for example, argued in a March 10, 2009, article on its Web site that transgender individuals would pose serious logistical problems for the military. In particular, the article suggests that housing for transgender people would be difficult and that women should not be forced to share housing with presurgical transgender people transitioning from male to female. The article also expresses concerns that some transgender people may teach in military schools and child-care centers and that this would be unfair to families "who are not comfortable" with transgender individuals.

Arguments surrounding transgender individuals in the military are similar to those about gays and lesbians serving in the military. The viewpoints in this book debates the issues in chapters titled What Are Current Attitudes Toward Gays in the Military? How Does "Don't Ask, Don't Tell" (DADT) Affect the Military? How Is the Government Handling the Issue of Gays in the Military? and How Do Other Countries Treat Gays in the Military? As one of the most important gay rights topics of the past few decades, the issue of gays in the military is likely to remain a source of controversy in the years to come.

CHAPTER 1

What Are Current Attitudes Toward Gays in the Military?

Chapter Preface

In the United States, attitudes toward gays and lesbians have shifted strongly over the past decades. During the middle part of the twentieth century, homosexuals faced serious prejudice. From the 1930s to the 1960s, "gay men and women were labeled 'deviants,' 'degenerate,' and 'sex criminals' by the medical profession, government officials, and the mass media," according to George Chauncey and colleagues in an August 2, 2003, article on the Web's History News Network. The article further notes that "Hollywood prohibited the discussion of gay issues or the appearance of gay or lesbian characters in its films, and many municipalities launched police campaigns to suppress gay life. The authorities worked together to create or reinforce the belief that gay people were an inferior class to be shunned by other Americans."

Since the 1950s, attitudes toward gays have changed drastically. Among the causes of this change have been "gays' own efforts, . . . the sexual revolution and the civil rights movements" according to a March 30, 2004, *Los Angeles Times* article by James Ricci and Patricia Ward Biederman. The same article notes that between 1977 and 2003, acceptance of gay elementary school teachers more than doubled, from 27 percent to 61 percent. In 1978, only 26 percent of respondents to a Gallup survey said that they would vote for a qualified gay candidate for president. By 1999, that number had increased to 59 percent.

In recent years acceptance of gay and lesbian relationships has continued to rise. According to a Gallup poll, in 2006, 39 percent of men and 49 percent of women characterized gay and lesbian relationships as morally acceptable. In 2010, the percentage had risen to 53 percent of men and 51 percent of women. The shift is especially noticeable among men eighteen to forty-nine years old, where there was a twenty-point leap, from 42 percent to 62 percent, among those saying that gay and lesbian relationships were morally acceptable. Lydia Saad, writing in a May 25, 2010, article on the Gallup Web site, concluded that "there is a gradual cultural shift under way in Americans' views toward gay individuals and gay rights. While public attitudes haven't moved consistently in gays' and lesbians' favor every year, the general trend is clearly in that direction."

The authors in this chapter debate how the change in attitudes toward gays and lesbians in general has affected the debate about gays in the military.

Editor's Note: "Don't Ask, Don't Tell was repealed by Congressional vote in December 2010. The policy remains in effect as of January 2011 until the President, the Secretary of Defense, and the Chairman of the Joint Chiefs of Staff certify that the implementation will not harm readiness, effectiveness, or recruitment and retention; formal repeal would then begin following a 60-day waiting period."

> *There appears to be a solid base of pub-*
> *lic support for a new policy that allows*
> *lesbian and gay Americans to serve*
> *their country without having to lie*
> *about who they are.*

Public Opinion Supports Allowing Gays in the Military

Anonymous

The author is a writer for the Canadian website Religious Tolerance. *In the following viewpoint, the anonymous author presents and analyzes data from opinion polls gauging levels of support for gays in the military. The author finds general increases in levels of support for gays in the military. Support appears to have risen even among groups generally thought of as opposing gays in the military, such as evangelical Christians and Republicans.*

As you read, consider the following questions:

1. According to the *Washington Post* polls, what was support for allowing gays and lesbians to openly serve in the military in 1993, 2001, and 2008?

Anonymous, "Polls Concerning Gays in the Military," *Religious Tolerance*, January 31, 2010. Reproduced by permission of the author.

2. In the *Zogby International* poll in 2006, how did U.S. military personnel respond to the question "Is a member of their unit homosexual?"

3. According to the 2009 Gallup poll, what groupings had less than 60 percent support for allowing openly gay men and women to serve in the military?

The most useful polls are longitudinal surveys continually taken repeatedly by the same polling agency over many years. They generally ask the same question each time, thus eliminating one problem associated with different questions used during polls taken by different companies.

The *Washington Post* has conducted such polls at approximately seven year intervals. They found that support for allowing gays and lesbians to openly serve in the military has risen markedly from the time that the DADT[1] policy was first introduced in 1993:

- 1993-MAY: 44% support, 55% oppose; 2% no opinion

- 2001-JAN: 61% support, 35% oppose; 3% no opinion

- 2008-JUL: 75% support, 22% oppose, 3% no opinion

The *Palm Center* describes themselves as ". . . a research institute of the University of California, Santa Barbara, committed to sponsoring state-of-the-art scholarship to enhance the quality of public dialogue about critical and controversial issues of the day."

They permitted Gregory M. Herek to place a guest post on their website in 2009-JUN. It contains the following graph, showing the trends in public opinion concerning repeal of the DADT policy.

Herek concluded:

"This is a policy area in which the public is ahead of Congress and the President. There will certainly be an outcry

---

1. DADT (Don't Ask, Don't Tell) is the U.S. military policy on gays and lesbians. Openly gay men and women are not allowed to serve in the military, but the military does not seek to actively uncover those who do not disclose their sexual orientation.

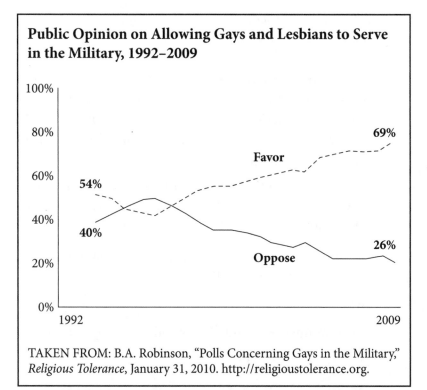

Public Opinion on Allowing Gays and Lesbians to Serve in the Military, 1992–2009

TAKEN FROM: B.A. Robinson, "Polls Concerning Gays in the Military," *Religious Tolerance*, January 31, 2010. http://religioustolerance.org.

from some far Right groups when President Obama suspends DADT and Congress overturns it permanently. In contrast to 1993, however, there appears to be a solid base of public support for a new policy that allows lesbian and gay Americans to serve their country without having to lie about who they are."

- 2000-JAN: *Fox News/Opinion Dynamics Poll* sampled 982 registered voters. The margin of error is ±3.0 percentage points. The question was: "One issue that has come up in the presidential debates is gays in the military. Do you think gay men and lesbians should be allowed to serve openly in the military?"

Results were:

- 57% supported gays serving openly;

- 30% were opposed;

- 13% were unsure.

- 2005-MAY: The *Boston Globe* sponsored a national poll conducted by the *New Hampshire Survey Center*. They polled 760 American adults between MAY-04 to 09. The margin of error is ±3.6 percentage points, and reported the results on 2005-MAY-15.

Most of the questions were related to same-sex marriage. However, they also asked about the military's exclusion of openly homosexual personnel. Results were:

- 79% of the subjects felt that gays and lesbians should be able to serve in the military.

- 18% were opposed.

- 4% were unsure or didn't respond.

The *Globe* reported that:

"Large majorities of Republicans, regular churchgoers, and people with negative attitudes toward gays think gays and lesbians should be allowed to serve openly in the military."

- 2006-OCT: Between OCT-24 and OCT-26, *Zogby International* polled 545 U.S. military personnel who have served in Iraq and Afghanistan. The margin of error is ±4.3 percentage points.

Results were:

- Is a member of their unit homosexual?

- 45% suspect one or more.

- 31% does not suspect any.

- 23% were definitely aware of one or more.

- 55% said that the presence of gays and lesbians is well known within their unit.

- Should gays and lesbians be allowed to serve?

- 37% disagreed

- 26% agreed

- About 75% felt comfortable around gays and lesbians

- 78% would join the military regardless of whether gays and lesbians were allowed to openly serve.

- 2007-MAY: A *CNN/Opinion Research Corp.* poll was held between MAY-04 and 06. The specific question was: "Do you think people who are openly gay or homosexual should or should not be allowed to serve in the U.S. military?"

Results were:

- 79% believe that openly gay people should be allowed to serve in the military

- 18% oppose openly gay persons in the military.

- 3% had no opinion or did not answer.

- 2008-JUL: A detailed Washington Post-ABC News poll was conducted between 2008-JUL-10 to 13 among 1,119 adults. The margin of error is ±3 percentage points. It is particularly interesting because the pollsters reported results as a function of religious and political party affiliation. Support for allowing gays and lesbians to serve openly was:

- 82% among Roman Catholics.

- Over 80% among women.

- Over 80% among Democrats.

- 80% among those with no declared religious affiliation.

- Over 75% among independents.

- 75% among the general population. This is an increase of 13 percentage points since early 2001.

- Over 2/3rds of men.

- 66% among Republicans (This is more than double the 1993 value of 32%).

- Almost 2/3rds among persons identifying themselves as conservatives.

- 57% among white evangelical Christians!!

- 2008-DEC-4: Princeton Survey Research Associates asked: "Do you think there should or should NOT be ... gays and lesbians serving openly in the military. Results were 66% in favor, 29% against. The margin of error is ±3.7 percentage points.

- 2008-DEC-21: A *CNN/Opinion Research Corp.* poll was held between DEC-19 and 21. Results were:

- 81% believe that openly gay people should be allowed to serve in the military

- 17% oppose openly gay persons in the military.

- 2% had no opinion or did not answer.

The question asked was: "Do you think people who are openly gay or homosexual should or should not be allowed to serve in the U.S. military?" We have never seen a poll on a question related to sex or morality in which the percentage of adults stating no opinion was so small.

The margin of error was ±3 percentage points.

- 2009-APR-27: A *Quinnipiac University* poll asked the question: "Federal law currently prohibits openly gay men and women from serving in the military. Do you think this law should be repealed or not?" They found

60% agreed and 36% disagreed. The question was asked after many questions relating to marriage and adoption by same-sex couples, so the earlier responses may have depressed the level of support for the abolition of DADT. The margin of error was ±2.2 percentage points.

- 2009-MAY: A *Gallup* poll revealed that support for an end to DADT has risen significantly since their earlier survey in 2004, from 63% to 69%. They asked the question: "Do you favor or oppose allowing openly gay men and lesbian women to serve in the military?"

The majority of every group sampled, including:

- Political conservatives moderates and liberals,

- Republicans, Democrats and Independents,

- Persons who attend church every week, most weeks, monthly, seldom and never, and

- Adults of all ages from 18 to 65+

favor repeal of DADT. 58% of Republicans, 57% of those from the U.S. South, 57% of those with a high-school education or less, and 58% of those describing themselves as political conservatives support allowing gays to openly serve. All of the other groupings had levels of support 60% or more.

The margin of error is ±3 percentage points.

> *"Many heterosexuals find homosexual behavior immoral and not conducive to [military] unit cohesion."*

Public Opinion Does Not Justify Allowing Gays in the Military

Cal Thomas

Cal Thomas is a conservative syndicated columnist and author. In the following viewpoint, he argues that the military should not be used as a test lab for social change, and that gay service members could hurt unit cohesion. He argues that rising public support for gay service members is the result of a lack of political leadership. He concludes that President Barack Obama did not win enough popular support in his election to give him a mandate for allowing gay men and women to serve openly in the military.

As you read, consider the following questions:

1. Where does Thomas say is the place to start in considering whether gays should be allowed to serve in the military?

2. How does the author say the armed services might be hurt if they were open to all behaviors?

3. Why does Thomas say few leaders wish to give voice to opposing points of view?

I am sympathetic to the story told by Joseph Rocha, who claims in a *Washington Post* opinion column that he was discharged from the Navy because he is gay, though he says he never told anyone. Mr. Rocha says his male colleagues concluded he was gay when he wouldn't laugh at their dirty jokes about women or visit prostitutes with them.

The Military Is Not a Lab

Gay service members have a point when they claim a double standard exists for heterosexuals and homosexuals regarding sexual behavior. Mr. Rocha also purports cover-ups by higher-ups about male sexual assaults on lesbians and the pressure he says lesbians feel to keep quiet because by "telling" they could face discharge.

But we are beginning in the wrong place. The place to start is whether citizens of this country, through their elected representatives and the military leaders named by them, have a right to determine what type of service members best serve the interests, safety and security of the United States. I contend we do. The military should not be a test lab. Pressure is building to put female sailors on submarines, along with gay, lesbian, bisexual and transgender people, presumably. That many heterosexuals find homosexual behavior immoral and not conducive to unit cohesion is of no concern to the social wrecking crew.

What gay activists apparently don't care about is the effect reshaping the military in their image would have on our ability to fight and defend the country, which, after all, is the purpose of a military. If the armed services were open to all behaviors (as distinct from orientations), recruitment might become more difficult. Some of the services have struggled recently to meet their recruitment goals, though overall enlistment is up because of the economy.

At the Human Rights Campaign dinner Saturday [October 2009] in Washington, President [Barack] Obama said, "I will end 'don't ask, don't tell.'" He also pledged to bring an end to the Defense of Marriage Act (DOMA), which was passed by a Republican Congress and signed by President [Bill] Clinton. Mr. Obama knows—or should know—that he does not have that power. He took an oath to faithfully execute the laws of the United States.

No Mandate for Change

If Congress wants to repeal DOMA and change the military's behavioral codes, it can do so through new legislation. But that would put Blue Dog [conservative] Democrats at risk at re-election time because they serve mostly conservative districts. They know their political careers would be over if they voted in favor of gay marriage or for gays in the military.

The gays-in-the-military and gay-marriage issues are part of a broader attempt by liberals to restructure society. Social activists despise biblical morality (which heterosexuals could use a little more, too), traditional values that have been proved to work when tried and numerous other cultural mores. This is not an opinion. It also is not a secret. The more radical activists have written and spoken openly about their intentions. Mr. Obama's language (whether action follows is another matter) gives lip service to their cause.

Opinion polls have shown the public shifting in favor of gays in the military, including a recent Gallup poll that found that "Americans are 6 percentage points more likely than they were four years ago to favor allowing openly gay men and lesbian women to serve in the military, 69 percent to 63 percent." That is mostly because there are few leaders who wish to give voice to opposing points of view. They fear being shouted down or accused of homophobia.

We will get more of what we tolerate. Sexual behavior is an important cultural and moral issue. Mr. Obama won the election with just 52 percent of the popular vote and a margin of 7 percent over Sen. John McCain. This should not be seen as a mandate for him and his administration to make over America in a secular and liberal image. Neither should it be seen as an invitation to give blanket approval to homosexuality, considered by some to be against the best interests of the people who practice it as well as the nations that accept it.

> *"A new poll ... found that a majority of active-duty service members want to keep the 'Don't Ask, Don't Tell' policy in place."*

Polled Military Personnel Do Not Support Gays in the Military

Dave Eberhart

Dave Eberhart is an author; he served in the U.S. Navy from 1963 to 1974. In the following viewpoint, he argues that most military personnel oppose repealing "Don't Ask, Don't Tell" (DADT). Moreoever, he says, the number of service members who might resign if DADT were repealed could seriously damage the armed forces. Eberhart notes that acceptance of gays in the military is increasing, however, and concludes that the fight to prevent the repeal of DADT is increasingly difficult.

As you read, consider the following questions:

1. According to Eberhart, how many service personnel would be lost if one in ten left because of the repeal of the DADT policy?

Dave Eberhart, "Military Opposes Obama's Pro-Gay Stance," *Newsmax*, January 8, 2009. Reproduced by permission.

2. What percentage of service members oppose the repeal of DADT, according to the author?

3. How many service members does the *Military Times*, as cited by Eberhart, say have been discharged because of DADT?

When Bill Clinton came to power [as U.S. president] in 1993, among his first agenda items: Allow gays to serve openly in the armed forces.

"Don't Ask, Don't Tell" Remains Best Policy

The plan sparked a firestorm of controversy, with Clinton ultimately acquiescing to what became known as the "Don't Ask, Don't Tell"[1] policy, a position military brass found acceptable.

Now, a new commander in chief is facing the same hot-button issue and critics from both the left and the right are already taking shots at President-elect Barack Obama's plans to deal with the matter. Most expect Obama, who pledged during the Democratic primaries to end "Don't Ask Don't Tell," to dispense with the rule and allow gays serving in the military to profess their homosexuality openly.

A new poll by the *Military Times*, however, found that a majority of active-duty service members want to keep the "Don't Ask, Don't Tell" policy in place.

Little surprise, then, that Obama appears increasingly reluctant to repeat Clinton's disastrous decision to tackle—right out of the starting blocks—the controversial issue of how to handle openly gay men and women serving in the military. That political wariness hasn't stopped some on the left from insisting that the new administration will give the demise of "Don't Ask, Don't Tell" top priority.

1. "Don't Ask, Don't Tell" is the U.S. military policy on gays and lesbians in the military. Openly gay men and women are not allowed to serve in the military, but the military does not actively seek to uncover those who do not disclose their sexual orientation.

In a few weeks, Rep. Ellen Tauscher, D-Calif., will reopen the issue by re-introducing legislation to repeal the 1993 law stating that homosexuals are not eligible to be in the military.

Elaine Donnelly, the founder and president of the Center for Military Readiness, which favors the ban on gays, says Clinton's effort to lift the ban was one of the most controversial agenda items of his administration—crippling his rapport with the military and contributing to the Democrats losing control of Congress in 1994.

"This time, the move to repeal the law is coming from Congress," she says. "Anybody who thinks that Obama's administration won't push for it is mistaken."

Perceptions purveyed in the media are less important than reality, and the meetings of high-level transition team members with representatives of the lesbian, gay, bisexual, and transgendered left are a clear indication that Obama's administration is fully engaged in this issue, Donnelly tells Newsmax.

"The only difference is that the meetings are taking place behind closed doors, instead of in the Oval Office with an official photograph taken and published in the *Washington Post*, as Clinton did in 1993," she adds.

But not all maneuvering is behind those closed doors.

The nation's largest gay-rights lobbying group has demanded that Obama eliminate the policy banning openly gays from the armed forces.

Last month [in December 2008], the Human Rights Campaign asked the president-elect to adopt the group's "Blueprint for Positive Change," which includes the banishment of the "Don't Ask, Don't Tell" policy.

According to a Human Rights Campaign official, the specific demand is to "develop a plan within the first 100 days to eliminate the military's . . . policy regarding the sexual orientation of its members."

Large Potential Losses

But Donnelly is having none of it, noting that the only change that can come about is negative and crippling rather than positive.

"The advocates of gays in the military at the *Military Times* spun their poll story by focusing on the 71 percent who said they would stay if the law is repealed, instead of the almost one in 10 who said they would definitely leave, plus an additional 14 percent who said they would consider leaving," she tells Newsmax. "Losses anywhere close to these numbers would virtually destroy the volunteer force."

Donnelly did the math:

- A rough estimate using Defense Department numbers for all service branches and components, totaling more than 2 million, indicates that a loss of one in ten (almost 10 percent) would cost the military approximately 228,600 people—more than the active duty Marine Corps (200,000).

- If an additional 14 percent decided to leave, the voluntary exodus would translate into a loss of almost 527,000—a figure approaching the size of today's active duty Army (more than 545,000).

"Estimates of losses in active duty forces alone would range between 141,000 (10 percent) and 323,000 (23 percent)," warns Donnelly.

The poll's findings are not an exact prediction, but they are significant and ought to be of concern to President Obama and members of Congress who are considering a vote to repeal the 1993 law, says Donnelly.

"This potential decimation of the volunteer force eclipses the small number of discharges that occurred over a period of nine years [under 'Don't Ask, Don't Tell']," concludes Donnelly.

Meanwhile as the controversy brews, the Obama transition camp may be leaving the new chief executive some wiggle room.

According to the *Washington Blade*, a newspaper serving the gay community, a member of the team is downplaying media reports that the president-elect has decided to delay efforts to repeal the law popularly called "Don't Ask, Don't Tell" until 2010.

The anonymous representative said the decision on how to deal with "Don't Ask, Don't Tell" would be tackled only after more experts have joined the Obama administration. "These decisions will not be made before the full national security team is in place," the spokesperson said.

Also weighing in on the timing of the fate of the law, the *Washington Times* recently reported that two people who have advised Obama's transition team said the president-elect "will not move for months, and perhaps not until 2010."

Meanwhile, Rep. Barney Frank, D-Mass., who is gay, said repealing "Don't Ask, Don't Tell" may be further off and told the *Blade* that "once Iraq is over," Congress can wipe the law off the books.

But Donnelly is not buying into Barney Frank's delayed-decision scenario.

She tells Newsmax, "The gay activists, including Barney Frank, keep telling conservative media that nothing will happen anytime soon. But a reporter for a liberal major media organization who had been surveying the same people was told that this is the number three item on their agenda. I believe that the liberal reporter is correct."

Donnelly concludes, "Keep in mind that Frank has threatened to cut the defense budget by 25 percent. All the pressure will be on the Joint Chiefs to go along with him in the 'best interests of the military.'"

Rep. Tauscher doesn't believe the wait will be long either, telling CNN recently that, in her opinion, the administration would approve of such a bill in 2009.

The Military Opposes Change

But whether sooner or later, the issue is one of the most charged the new president will have to confront.

Adding to the rising temperature in the pressure cooker is the recent 2008 annual *Military Times* poll of active duty personnel that reveals most active-duty service members continue to oppose Obama's campaign pledge to end the "Don't Ask, Don't Tell" policy to allow gays to serve openly in the military.

According to that poll, approximately 58 percent of respondents are opposed to efforts to repeal the 1993 law. This level of solid support for the law has remained virtually unchanged in similar annual surveys dating back to January 2005.

According to a report in the *Military Times*, Army Capt. Steven J. Lacy, a logistician assigned to the 71st Transportation Battalion at Fort Eustis, Va., said he is very concerned about the policy being repealed.

"I think a lot of people are," Lacy said. "In the field environment, you're in very close proximity to one another. The fact that someone could be openly gay could exacerbate stress on teams and small units when you're already at a high stress level."

Donnelly agrees.

If Congress repeals the 1993 statute stating that homosexuals are not eligible to serve in uniform, and the military is ordered to accommodate professed (not discreet) homosexuals, the culture of the military will be radically changed, she argues.

"Recruiters will be directed to accept and even seek out professed homosexuals for induction in all branches of the military, including direct ground combat communities.

"This means that heterosexuals—the majority of men and women who volunteer to serve—will be required to live in forced cohabitation with professed, not discreet, homosexuals, on all military bases and ships at sea, on a 24/7 basis.

"Such a policy would impose new, unneeded burdens of sexual tension on men and women serving in high-pressure working conditions, far from home, that are unlike any occupation in the civilian world.

"The real-world issue here is not superficial. Nor is it a Hollywood fantasy portrayed for laughs in a television sitcom. We are talking about human sexuality and the normal, human desire for personal privacy and modesty in sexual matters.

"Repealing the 1993 law would be tantamount to forcing female soldiers to cohabit with men in intimate quarters, on all military bases and ships at sea, on a 24/7 basis," she concludes.

Uphill Battle

But Donnelly may be bucking a strong current for change.

That same *Military Times* poll highlighted above indicates that 71 percent of respondents said they would continue to serve if the policy was overturned.

Sgt. 1st Class Joseph Pfau, of the 284th Engineer Company in Seagoville, Texas, told the *Times* he isn't concerned about the issue.

"That policy does not bother me whatsoever," Pfau said. "I don't judge people by their sexual orientation. I judge them by the kind of person they are. As long as they do their job, it does not bother me."

But it's not just the lower ranks that are getting more comfortable with gays openly in the military.

Retired Admiral Charles Larson, former Superintendent of the U.S. Naval Academy, heads a list of 104 retired generals and admirals calling for an end to the military's "Don't Ask, Don't Tell" policy, the Associated Press reported.

In a petition, Larson and the others respectfully call for the repeal of the "Don't Ask, Don't Tell" policy:

"Those of us endorsing this letter have dedicated our lives to defending the rights of our citizens to believe whatever they wish. Scholarly data shows there are approximately one million gay and lesbian veterans in the United States today, as well as 65,000 gays and lesbians currently serving in our armed forces.

"They have served our nation honorably. We support the recent comments of former Chairman of the Joint Chiefs, General John Shalikashvili, who has concluded that repealing the . . . policy would not harm and would indeed help our armed forces."

For her part, Donnelly admits the battle may be uphill.

Activists for gays in the military are not letting up in their drive to impose their agenda on the military, she says.

Joe Solmonese, president of the Human Rights Campaign, said transition leaders were "very receptive" to requests from gay activists. "I think they went to great lengths to explain their vision for how [policy initiatives] would work and how our community would be a part of that," he told the *Washington Blade*.

According to a *Military Times* report, the DoD [Department of Defense] has discharged nearly 12,500 service members since the law was first enforced in 1994, including critically needed service members such as Arabic linguists, medics, pilots and intelligence analysts.

Donnelly opines that the number of such discharges under "Don't Ask, Don't Tell" could be nearly wiped out if induction forms asked a question about sexual preference right up front.

Interestingly, if that question was allowed to be asked and other key features of the old law stayed in effect, a "yes" answer might not result in a kneejerk tossing of the application.

Donnelly notes to Newsmax: "It's technical, but there is the 'rebuttable presumption' language, which applies only if someone said they were gay under unusual circumstances; i.e., while drunk, trying to get out of the military, etc. It's a long story, but it is not the loophole that it appears to be."

> *"The current poll . . . not only may suffer from the same selection biases contained in the previous poll, but worse, it contains questions that put a negative slant on gays serving in the military."*

A Poll Showing Lack of Support for Gays in the Military Is Flawed

Alan M. Steinman

Alan M. Steinman is a retired rear admiral with the United States Public Health Service and the U.S. Coast Guard, and the former surgeon general of the Coast Guard. In the following viewpoint he argues that a poll by the Military Times *measuring levels of support for gays in the military among service personnel is biased. Steinman notes that the poll is tilted toward older service members, that it asks questions that negatively portray gays in the military, and that it fails to ask whether service members already know gay men and women serving in their units.*

As you read, consider the following questions:

1. What percentage of respondents in the earlier *Military Times* poll were junior active duty troops, and why does Steinman believe this is a problem?
2. Who was Eric Alva, according to the author?
3. What does Steinman believe the Pentagon should do to find out about troop attitudes toward gays in the military?

A new poll of subscribers to the various *Military Times* publications (e.g., *Army Times, Navy Times*, etc.) may have enough selection bias and negatively biased questions towards gays serving in the military that it will likely provide support for those who do not want Don't Ask, Don't Tell (DADT)[1] repealed.

A Biased Poll

The new poll, currently being conducted [in 2009], follows on the heels of last year's poll of *Military Times* subscribers which purportedly showed that a majority of active duty members didn't want DADT repealed, and also showed a small percentage of active duty members who said they would not reenlist if DADT were repealed. That previous poll suffered from extreme selection bias in that it did not survey a random sample of active duty military, but instead, it apparently sampled only subscribers to the *Military Times* publications. Furthermore, the responses represented only those who chose to participate, creating yet another source of selection bias. Finally, there was no attempt to adjust the responses so that they more closely resembled the age/rank/service affiliation of active duty troops. Since *Military Times* subscribers tend to be more senior in age and rank, the responses reflected primarily the opinions of senior military members, and then only of those who chose to

1. DADT is the U.S. military policy on gays and lesbians in the military. Openly gay men and women may not serve in the military, but the military does not actively investigate people's sexual orientation.

reply. As a result, only about 5% of the responses were from junior active duty troops ... despite the fact that these members comprise a large percentage of the active duty workforce.

Nonetheless, the negative findings from that previous poll got great media attention, despite the *Military Times* disclaimer at the end of the poll admitting that it did not represent an accurate view of the active duty workforce.

The current poll is even worse, since it not only may suffer from the same selection biases contained in the previous poll, but worse, it contains questions that put a negative slant on gays serving in the military. Furthermore, the demographic information contained in the poll asks not only the usual identifiers of age, rank, gender, service affiliation, etc., but shockingly, it asks people to identify their sexual orientation! To be sure, respondents have the option to "decline to answer," but realistically, how many gay, lesbian or bisexual [GLB] active duty troops will be stupid enough to self-identity themselves in a poll sent specifically to them by name, and which includes a request for their name, address and telephone number (so that they can be contacted if they win a sweepstakes award (an inducement to encourage participation in the poll)?! I would be most surprised if the poll finds any active duty gay, lesbian or bisexual respondents, leading to the problem that some unscrupulous opponents of gays serving honorably in the military might argue that since there are so few GLB members on active duty, as reflected by this poll, why bother worrying about DADT at all?

Gays Portrayed Negatively in Poll

Regarding the potential negative bias, the very first question following the demographics asks respondents if they've ever been hit on by someone of the same gender, and follows that by asking what their reaction was to that? Notably, though, the poll does not ask respondents about being hit on by a member of the opposite sex. I imagine many female active duty personnel would be interested in that data, since that situation is all too common in the military today, yet it is ignored by the *Military Times* poll. We will thus have data only on presumably unwelcome gay/lesbian sexual advances, but there will be no comparative data on unwelcome straight sexual advances. This constitutes an obvious negative spin to gay military service, focusing only on apparent gay misconduct.

Then the poll proceeds to ask respondents if their superiors ever knew about a gay service member but refused to do anything about that situation? You can easily see the negative bias in the way this question is worded as well. It and the previous question inferring gay/lesbian misconduct play to the fear that gays serving openly will misbehave and create disruption in the unit; and further, commands may not be doing anything about gays serving (presumably openly and thus illegally). And the questions appear first in the order of opinion responses sought from subscribers, thus potentially generating a negative connotation about gays in the military even before asking opinions about gays serving honestly and honorably.

In another example of a negative bias against gays, the poll asks if the DADT policy were repealed, should there be certain jobs from which known homosexuals should be barred? And then it gives some "helpful" examples like submarines, special operations or drill instructor. The premise of this question is that gays are unqualified for certain military ratings, perhaps because their "macho" peers might be discomforted by their presence. Is there some objective reason for asking this question? Never mind that SSGT [staff sergeant] Eric Alva, USMC [U.S. Marine Corps], was known to be gay by others in his unit when they went into battle the first day of the Iraq War (and Alva became the first casualty of that war). And never mind that nuclear submariner Steve Lorandos was known to be gay by everyone on his boat and there was no problem

Military Times Poll Was Misleading

In December 2008, a *Military Times* poll found that 58% of U.S. troops do not want gays and lesbians to serve openly in the armed forces. Subsequently, some experts have concluded that the "don't ask, don't tell" policy should not be repealed, because ... 10% of [troops] say they would consider leaving the armed forces if the ban were lifted. ...

[However], there is a significant gap between attitudes and behavior—what people believe, and how they behave. In the 1970s, far more than ten percent of officers said they would leave the service if women were admitted to West Point. ... But when integration became a reality, there was no mass exodus; the opinions turned out to be just opinions.

Nathaniel Frank, Palm Center,
January 13, 2009. www.palmcenter.org.

with unit morale, unit cohesion or with the sub's combat readiness. And never mind that Marine Corps aircrewman Brian Fricke was known to be gay by his fellow Marines. And never mind that I have personally spoken to openly gay infantry men and artillery men at Fort Lewis during my lectures at college classes on base there, and all state that there are no problems with their battle buddies in combat arms. Should all of these talented, experienced gay troops have been barred from the jobs in which they contributed to the national defense, simply because they're gay?

Experts Agree Poll Is Biased

Two academic institutions which have expertise in designing and interpreting polls agree that biased wording of some of the new poll's questions is problematical. In an editorial titled "Scholars Question Methodology of New Poll on Gay Troops," the Palm Center of the University of California, Santa Barbara stated the following:

> Researchers are particularly concerned about the potential for response bias, a phenomenon that can occur when questions are not worded or arranged neutrally. After a number of questions about the respondent's age and rank, the *Military Times* survey poses questions about sexual advances by gay troops, and follows those by asking about attitudes toward "don't ask, don't tell." Professor Aaron Belkin said that by prompting respondents to link sexual predation with the gays-in-the-military issue, the survey may generate misleading results. "If you set up a scenario about sexual predation and then ask someone how they feel about gays in the military, you can predict the response is not going to be positive." (Belkin is associate professor of political science and director of the Palm Center at the University of California, Santa Barbara.)

In addition, the Williams Institute of the University of California, Los Angeles stated the following:

> Dr. Gary Gates said that on hot-button emotional issues like gay rights, "survey researchers must pay particular attention to framing their questions in neutral ways." Gates is a co-author of a report just released in conjunction with the Williams Institute which addresses how the "potentially stigmatizing nature of some of the questions surrounding sexual orientation" can bias responses. (Gates is Williams distinguished scholar at the Williams Institute at the UCLA School of Law, and the report is titled, "Best Practices for Asking Questions about Sexual Orientation on Surveys.")

Finally, Dr. Nathaniel Frank, author of the most comprehensive text ever published on gays in the military, *Unfriendly Fire: How the Gay Ban Undermines the Military and Weakens America*, stated:

Dr. Nathaniel Frank, senior research fellow at the Palm Center, said the relevant question is not what the troops want, but whether they are capable of serving with gays without becoming undisciplined. "From a poll that does ask the right questions, we've learned that three quarters of troops are comfortable around gay people and that two thirds already know or suspect gays in their units," he said, referring to a 2006 Zogby poll of troops returning from Iraq and Afghanistan.

The Most Important Question

The new *Military Times* poll fails to ask the most relevant question of all, and that is: are there known gays serving alongside their straight peers? Since operational readiness is known to be excellent, and since our military is currently considered the finest, the most battle-ready and most combat experienced in the world, if known gays are serving now, in both theaters of war, where are all the assumed problems that formed the foundation for DADT? Where are all the problems with unit morale, unit cohesion and combat readiness? The primary assumption underlying the DADT law was that any known gay in a unit would seriously discomfort heterosexuals in the unit and thus degrade operational readiness. One would think that a fair poll of active duty troop opinion would attempt to measure this critical factor, as other polls of military opinion have successfully done.

The 2006 Zogby Poll specifically asked about known gays serving in a unit. The results showed that 23% of U.S. veterans of the Iraq/Afghanistan Wars knew for certain there were gays in their own unit, and that the majority of them stated that this fact was widely known by others in their unit. Furthermore, another 45% of these Iraq/Afghanistan War veterans stated that they suspected there were gays in their own unit. And 73% of the troops said they were comfortable working with gays and lesbians. Again, with tens of thousands of straight troops indicating they either know for certain or suspect there are gays in their own unit, where are all the problems? Since evidently the problems are few, if any, how can anyone justify keeping DADT and discharging competent, trained and experienced gay and lesbian troops if they are not negatively impacting operational effectiveness?

The problem with the current *Military Times* poll, if its results indeed prove to suffer from selection bias and if indeed the results purport to demonstrate a negative view of gays serving in the military (based on questions that support negative views of gay service members), is its potential to influence decision makers in the Pentagon and in Congress. Hopefully these leaders will be aware of the problems with any poll conducted in an unscientific manner and whose results therefore cannot be said to accurately reflect the opinion of the active duty workforce.

Ideally, the Pentagon should conduct its own research on this issue through statistically valid polls which contain only unbiased questions. I would love to see an updated version of the Zogby Poll conducted in which the troops are again queried on their knowledge of serving with gay, lesbian or bisexual peers. If, as I suspect, there is an even higher percentage than in the previous poll of troops serving with known gay, lesbian or bisexual peers, and if indeed the Pentagon can verify that there are no demonstrable problems with unit morale, unit cohesion and combat readiness, despite the known presence of gay troops, then that should herald the end of DADT. If the Pentagon won't or can't conduct such a poll, perhaps a group of interested independent agencies could jointly sponsor and fund a scientifically valid poll of the active duty troops. At the very least, it might provide a more realistic view of gays serving in the military than is likely to result from the current *Military Times* poll.

Periodical and Internet Sources Bibliography

The following articles have been selected to supplement the diverse views presented in this chapter.

Elisabeth Bumiller	"In Military, New Debate over Policy Toward Gays," *New York Times*, April 30, 2009. www.nytimes.com.
Mike Daniels	"Majority of Americans Favor Allowing Openly-Gay Military Service," *Secular News Daily*, May 31, 2010. www.secularnewsdaily .com.
Elaine Donnelly	"Poll on Gays in the Military Perturbs Palm Center," Center for Military Readiness, January 14, 2009. www.cmrlink.org.
Nathaniel Frank	"*Military Times* Poll Flawed," Palm Center, January 13, 2009. www.palmcenter.org.
Kevin Hechtkopf	"Support for Gays in the Military Depends on the Question," CBS News, February 11, 2010. www.cbsnews.com.
Hillary May	"Poll: Gays in Military Not Congress Decision," *Washington Times*, May 25, 2010. www.washing tontimes.com.
Mike Mokrzycki	"Support for Gays in the Military Crosses Ideological, Party Lines," ABC News, February 12, 2010. http://abcnews.go.com.
Ed O'Keefe and Jennifer Agiesta	"75% Back Letting Gays Serve Openly," *Washington Post*, February 12, 2010. www.washing tonpost.com.
USA Today	"Military Poll Shows Less Opposition to Gays Serving Openly," February 5, 2010. http:// content.usatoday.com.

OPPOSING
VIEWPOINTS®
SERIES

CHAPTER 2

How Does "Don't Ask, Don't Tell" (DADT) Affect the Military?

Chapter Preface

Some commentators have argued that the Don't Ask, Don't Tell (DADT) policy that prevents gays and lesbians from openly serving in the military contributes to the sexual harassment of women in the military. Thus, in an article on its website, the National Organization for Women argues that "DADT is used against women in the practice known as lesbian baiting. Military women are intimidated into unwanted sexual intercourse, and if they refuse, they are threatened with being outed as lesbians."

J. Jennings Moss in a February 4, 1997, article in the *Advocate* examined the link between lesbian baiting and sexual harassment more extensively. Jennings points to the case of Amy Barnes, who refused to talk to a male sailor, prompting an investigation that led to her discharge under DADT. Barnes was not alone; Jennings reported that many women in the military had their sexual orientation investigated after they reported sexual harassment. "The gay policy gives men in the military a tool to extort sexual compliance from women under the threat of calling them lesbians. If a woman reports sexual harassment or rape, they very frequently experience retaliation by the perpetrators, who accuse them of being gay," according to Michelle Benecke of the anti-DADT group Servicemembers Legal Defense Network.

The practice of lesbian baiting may help to explain the fact that DADT has had a greater impact on women than on men, according to a January 5, 2003, report by Human Rights Watch. The report notes that in 2001 women accounted for only 14 percent of the armed forces, but for fully 30 percent of discharges under Don't Ask, Don't Tell. The figures continued to be disproportionately high in subsequent years. In 2008, "women accounted for 34 percent of the discharges but comprised 14 percent of the military," according to Bonnie Erbe in a June 1, 2010, article on the Politics Daily Web site.

The Center for Military Readiness, on the other hand, has argued that the incidence of sexual harassment in the military is exaggerated and that unfounded accusations of harassment may harm the armed forces. "Extremism in the prosecution of men is not necessarily helpful to women," according to a January 13, 2006, article on the center's Web site. The article also suggests that the main problem in the military is not harassment, but the fact that allowing women in the military undermines correct gender relations. Women in the military have undermined the idea of a "lady," which, according to the article, "makes it harder to understand the meaning of 'officer and gentleman.'"

The viewpoints in this chapter examine other effects of the DADT policy on morale, readiness, retention of soldiers, and incidents of harassment.

Editor's Note: "Don't Ask, Don't Tell was repealed by Congressional vote in December 2010. The policy remains in effect as of January 2011 until the President, the Secretary of Defense, and the Chairman of the Joint Chiefs of Staff certify that the implementation will not harm readiness, effectiveness, or recruitment and retention; formal repeal would then begin following a 60-day waiting period."

> *"Open homosexuality is incompatible with military service because it undermines the military ethos upon which success in war ultimately depends."*

Repealing DADT Would Hurt Military Morale

Mackubin Thomas Owens

Mackubin Thomas Owens, a U.S. Marine veteran of the Vietnam War, is associate dean at the Naval War College and a contributing editor to National Review. *In the following viewpoint, he argues that allowing gays to serve openly in the military would undermine unit cohesion and morale. Owens contends that unit effectiveness is based on nonsexual brotherly bonds between those facing danger together and that tension and favoritism among gay service members would undermine those bonds. He concludes that military effectiveness demands that openly gay men and women be kept from serving in the military.*

As you read, consider the following questions:

1. According to Owens, what common-sense observation is reflected in the 1993 DADT law?

2. How does the author define *philia*?

3. How does Owens say that *eros* manifest itself, and what effect does he think that would have on the military?

As expected, President [Barack] Obama pledged during his [2010] State of the Union address to "work with Congress and our military to finally repeal the law that denies gay Americans the right to serve the country they love because of who they are." This law—often mistakenly referred to as "don't ask, don't tell"—was passed in 1993 by a veto-proof margin in a Democratic controlled Congress.

Gays Threaten Unit Cohesion

The law codified regulations in effect before President Bill Clinton's inauguration [in 1993], making the historical prohibition against military service for homosexuals a matter of statute. As Secretary of Defense Robert Gates observed in June of last year [2009], "What we have is a law, not a policy or regulation. And as I discovered when I got into it, it is a very prescriptive law. It doesn't leave a lot to the imagination or a lot of flexibility."

The congressional findings supporting the 1993 law (section 654 of title 10, United States Code) reflect the common-sense observation that military organizations exist to win wars. To maximize the chances of battlefield success, military organizations must overcome the paralyzing effects of fear on the individual soldier and what the famous Prussian war theorist Carl von Clausewitz called "friction" and the "fog of uncertainty."

This they do by means of an ethos that stresses discipline, morale, good order and unit cohesion. Anything that threatens the nonsexual bonding that lies at the heart of unit cohesion adversely affects morale, discipline and good order, generating friction and undermining this ethos. Congress at the time and many today, including members of the military and

Opposition to Gays in the Military Is Not Bigotry

Some critics of my piece [opposing gays in the military] simply accused me of bigotry. . . . In fact my late brother was homosexual. I never stopped loving him because of his homosexuality and got along fine with him and his friends. . . .

I am as opposed to bigotry as anyone. Homosexuals should and do possess the equal civil rights of their fellow citizens. But there is no "right" to serve in the military, and there, effectiveness should trump all other considerations.

Mackubin Thomas Owens, National Review, *February 9, 2010.*

members of Congress from both parties, believe that service by open homosexuals poses such a threat.

There are many foolish reasons to exclude homosexuals from serving in the armed services. One is simple antihomosexual bigotry. But as the late Charles Moskos, the noted military sociologist, observed during the Clinton years, this does not mean that we should ignore the good ones. And the most important is expressed in the 1993 law: that open homosexuality is incompatible with military service because it undermines the military ethos upon which success in war ultimately depends.

Winning the nation's wars is the military's functional imperative. Indeed, it is the only reason for a liberal society to maintain a military organization. War is terror. War is confusion. War is characterized by chance, uncertainty and friction. The military's ethos constitutes an evolutionary response to these factors—an attempt to minimize their impact.

Philia vs. Eros

Accordingly, the military stresses such martial virtues as courage, both physical and moral, a sense of honor and duty, discipline, a professional code of conduct, and loyalty. It places a premium on such factors as unit cohesion and morale. The glue of the military ethos is what the Greeks called *philia*—friendship, comradeship or brotherly love. Philia, the bond among disparate individuals who have nothing in common but facing death and misery together, is the source of the unit cohesion that most research has shown to be critical to battlefield success.

Philia depends on fairness and the absence of favoritism. Favoritism and double standards are deadly to philia, and its associated phenomena—cohesion, morale and discipline—are absolutely critical to the success of a military organization.

The presence of open homosexuals in the close confines of ships or military units opens the possibility that *eros*—which unlike philia is sexual, and therefore individual and exclusive—will be unleashed into the environment. Eros manifests itself as sexual competition, protectiveness and favoritism, all of which undermine the nonsexual bonding essential to unit cohesion, good order, discipline and morale.

As Sen. James Webb (D., Va.), who was awarded the Navy Cross for valor as a Marine officer in Vietnam, wrote in the *Weekly Standard* in 1997, "There is no greater or more natural bias than that of an individual toward a beloved. And few emotions are more powerful, or more distracting, than those surrounding the pursuit of, competition for, or the breaking off of amorous relationships."

The destructive impact of such relationships on unit cohesion can be denied only by ideologues. Does a superior order his or her beloved into danger? If he or she demonstrates favoritism, what is the consequence for unit morale and discipline? What happens when jealousy rears its head? These are questions of life and death, and they help to explain why open homosexuality and homosexual behavior traditionally have been considered incompatible with military service.

Although it is popular to equate opposition to permitting homosexuals to serve openly in the military today with opposition to racial integration of the services six decades ago, the similarities between the two cases are superficial.

Former Chairman of the Joint Chiefs of Staff, Gen. Colin Powell, who no doubt knows something about racial discrimination, made the proper distinction in a reply to former Rep. Pat Schroeder during testimony before the House Armed Services Committee in 1992 when she argued that point. "Skin color is a benign nonbehavioral characteristic. Sexual orientation is perhaps the most profound of human behavioral characteristics. Comparison of the two is a convenient but invalid argument," he said.

The reason for excluding open homosexuals from the military has nothing to do with equal rights or freedom of expression. Indeed, there is no constitutional right to serve in the military. The primary consideration must be military effectiveness. Congress should keep the ban in place. It certainly should not change the law when the United States is engaged in two wars.

> "Open service doesn't disrupt this foundation ... because the 'band of brothers' mythos is based less on heterosexual backslapping than a shared sense of mission, honor, and duty."

Repealing DADT Would Not Hurt Morale

Charles McLean and P.W. Singer

Charles McLean is a federal executive fellow at the Brookings Institution and a lieutenant colonel in the U.S. Marine Corps. P.W. Singer is director of the 21st Century Defense Initiative at the Brookings Institution. In the following viewpoint, the authors argue that the military will have little trouble adapting to the repeal of Don't Ask, Don't Tell. The authors point to foreign militaries that allow gay troops to serve openly as evidence. The transition of the British Royal Navy to an open service was easy to implement and swiftly returned to normal. The authors argue that the benefit to the United States lagging behind other nations in terms of open service in the military is that we now know how to transition successfully.

As you read, consider the following questions:

1. How many of the United States' allies have transitioned to an open military, according to the article?
2. What do many critics of the repeal of Don't Ask, Don't Tell fear?
3. What does our allies' experience with the transition to open military suggest?

Every gay-pride parade seems to have its share of sailor suits, aviator sunglasses, and camouflage trousers. In the U.S., such costumes are often drawn from the Halloween bin, since gays cannot serve openly in the military, let alone march for pride in their official uniforms. But that's not the case in Britain, where gay members of the Royal Navy, Air Force, Army, and Marines not only march but also move their partners into the military's family housing. The armed forces has also embraced the shift—which came following a European Court of Human Rights ruling 1999—placing recruitment ads in gay publications, and, last summer, featuring an openly gay soldier on the cover of the military's official magazine.

Britain isn't the only U.S. ally to allow open gays in the military. More than 25 of our allies, including every original NATO [North Atlantic Treaty Organization] signatory other than the U.S. and Turkey, have transitioned to an open military. Most have made the switch since 1993, when Congress passed "don't ask, don't tell" (DADT), a policy that forbids gay soldiers from coming out of the closet. Last month Congress struck a compromise that could repeal DADT as early as this summer [2010]. But no matter when it happens—if it happens—the transition will be a matter of feverish debate. Critics have already warned that openly gay soldiers will sink morale—causing resignations, discord, and infighting—and ultimately damage readiness at a time when the U.S. military is already taxed to the extreme.

If the experience of our allies is any guide, however, the critics are wrong. In Britain, Australia, Canada, Israel, the Netherlands, and Sweden—strategic partners, often with militaries that have served alongside U.S. forces—the big news was well no news at all. Their transitions to open service were remarkably boring. "It was a nonevent," says retired Maj. Gen. Simon Willis, the former head of personnel for the Australian Defence Force, "and it continues to be a nonevent." Last month the Brookings Institution, in partnership with the Palm Center, a think tank at the University of California, Santa Barbara, brought Willis and other allied officers and experts together to discuss lessons learned from allowing openly gay service people. What they said should be a welcome source of comfort, mixed with caution, as the U.S. takes its first wobbly steps toward integration.

Open Service Is Easy to Implement

Above all, Congress and the Pentagon should rest assured that open service is, ironically, easier to implement than it is to study. Our allies had similarly fierce public debates. But once the new policies were in place, the return to normalcy was swift and all-encompassing. It was "really, really dull," recalls Craig Jones, a retired lieutenant commander in the British Royal Navy.

It helped, of course, that few pre-transition fears ever materialized. Cohesion within the ranks, for one, never faltered, and morale remained high. This shouldn't have surprised the international brass: for more than 3,000 years militaries have molded very different people into effective fighting units, says retired Capt. Alan Okros, a Canadian naval officer turned military scholar. Open service doesn't disrupt this foundation, he believes, because the "band of brothers" mythos is based less on heterosexual backslapping than a shared sense of mission, honor, and duty. As a result, none of our allies felt the need to build separate facilities for gay soldiers, and few straight soldiers seemed to notice a change in their personal space (or at least their perception of it). Privacy, it seems, matters more to culture warriors than to genuine warriors, who don't tend to expect a room of one's own in the first place.

Another key anxiety—or at least a perennial fear raised by some critics—was that an open military would be awash in rainbow décor, incidents of homosexual rape, and violent clashes between gay and straight soldiers. "There were concerns in the late '90s of gay men walking across the gangplank in feather boas and high heels," Jones remembers. "That just did not happen." On the contrary, gay soldiers were slow to identify themselves; when they did, they certainly didn't broadcast the news from every steeple and force themselves on their comrades. Equally muted was the response from straight soldiers—no nation recorded any significant rise in incidents—and military chaplains, who saw their role as serving all members regardless of their faith or sexuality. "People didn't leave the Canadian military," says Maj. Gen. Walter Semianiw, who commanded Canada's forces in Afghanistan and is now in charge of military personnel matters. "They just got on with the new policy."

Gay Rights Around the World

Perhaps Congress will get on with it as well. DADT has drummed out more than 13,000 soldiers and put thousands of others under incalculable stress. At a time when the mental health of U.S. troops is carefully monitored, its repeal should be seen as a matter of battle readiness, according to our allies. "Forcing [gay service men and women] to have to constantly censor themselves, to regulate their behavior, to pretend to be somebody they're not, is putting people at risk," says Okros, the retired Canadian captain. It's also hampering joint appointments, according to Canadian Navy Cmdr. Luc Cassivi,

Chairman of the Joint Chiefs Supports Repeal

As a murmur swept through a [Senate] hearing room packed with gay rights leaders, Admiral [Mike] Mullen said it was his personal belief that "allowing gays and lesbians to serve openly would be the right thing to do."

He is the first sitting chairman of the Joint Chiefs to support a repeal of the policy.

Elisabeth Bumiller, "Top Defense Official Seeks to End 'Don't Ask, Don't Tell,'" New York Times, *February 3, 2010. www.nytimes.com.*

who says that allied soldiers have turned down U.S. postings rather than return to the closet under DADT.

Fortunately, as a benefit of lagging behind our allies, we already know the basics of a successful transition. Most of the steps are obvious (leadership must set the tone; conduct standards and personnel policies must not single out any one minority). But other ideas cut across our instincts. Rather than a deliberative transition, our allies' experience suggests the shift should be done quickly; rather than surveying soldiers' attitudes on gay service, the repeal of DADT should be done top-down and authoritatively; above all, our review of the issue should be placed in the context of broader personnel concerns such as diversity and sexual harassment. "One thing I recommend not to do," says Danny Kaplan, who has studied the acceptance of gay soldiers in the Israeli Defense Forces, is "write a survey on which the title is 'Homosexuality in the American Military.'" Something for the Pentagon to keep in mind, it seems, as it compiles its report on the steps needed to prepare for the change. It's due by December 2010—plenty of time to think of a title.

> "Don't Ask, Don't Tell [is] an immoral law and policy that forces American soldiers to deceive and lie."

DADT Undermines the Honor of the Army

Daniel Choi

Daniel Choi is a former American infantry officer, veteran of the Iraq War, and a gay rights activist. In the following viewpoint, taken from an open letter to the president of the United States and every member of Congress, Choi argues that as a soldier he is duty-bound to honesty. He says that lying about his sexual identity goes against his honor and integrity. He notes in addition that soldiers who served under him knew he was gay and that they treated him no differently because they were professionals. He argues that to fire him is a slur on the professionalism of his fellow soldiers and subordinates. He urges the president and Congress to repeal Don't Ask, Don't Tell immediately.

As you read, consider the following questions:

1. According to Choi, what was demanded by the Cadet Honor Code?

2. What does the author say is the foundation of unit cohesion?

Daniel Choi, "Gay Soldier: Don't Fire Me," *amFix*, May 11, 2009. Reproduced by permission of the author.

3. What does Choi say he did after publicly announcing he was gay?

I have learned many lessons in the ten years since I first raised my right hand at the United States Military Academy at West Point and committed to fighting for my country. The lessons of courage, integrity, honesty and selfless service are some of the most important.

At West Point, I recited the Cadet Prayer every Sunday. It taught us to "choose the harder right over the easier wrong" and to "never be content with a half truth when the whole can be won." The Cadet Honor Code demanded truthfulness and honesty. It imposed a zero-tolerance policy against deception, or hiding behind comfort.

Following the Honor Code never bowed to comfortable timing or popularity. Honor and integrity are 24-hour values. That is why I refuse to lie about my identity.

I have personally served for a decade under Don't Ask, Don't Tell:[1] an immoral law and policy that forces American soldiers to deceive and lie about their sexual orientation. Worse, it forces others to tolerate deception and lying. These values are completely opposed to anything I learned at West Point. Deception and lies poison a unit and cripple a fighting force.

As an infantry officer, an Iraq combat veteran and a West Point graduate with a degree in Arabic, I refuse to lie to my commanders. I refuse to lie to my peers. I refuse to lie to my subordinates. I demand honesty and courage from my soldiers. They should demand the same from me.

I am committed to applying the leadership lessons I learned at West Point. With 60 other LGBT [lesbian, gay, bisexual, and transgender] West Point graduates, I helped form our organization, Knights Out, to fight for the repeal of this

"Don't Ask, Don't Tell" is the military policy that prevents openly gay men and women from serving in the military. The policy likewise dictates that the military cannot ask about service members' sexual identity.

Gay Soldiers Deserve Equal Rights

[Congressman Joe Sestak:] Look, I went to war, and we knew by survey that when I went to war that we had a certain percentage in that carrier battle group, and when I was on the ground briefly in Afghanistan, that were gay. And now we come back to America and say they don't have equal rights. I've never understood it. This is something where we have to correct this. It's just not right.

Huffington Post, *May 7, 2009. www.huffingtonpost.com.*

discriminatory law and educate cadets and soldiers after the repeal occurs. When I receive emails from deployed soldiers and veterans who feel isolated, alone, and even suicidal because the torment of rejection and discrimination, I remember my leadership training: soldiers cannot feel alone, especially in combat. Leaders must reach out. They can never diminish the fighting spirit of a soldier by tolerating discrimination and isolation. Leaders respect the honor of service. Respecting each soldier's service is my personal promise.

Discharge

The Department of the Army sent a letter discharging me on April 23rd [2009]. I will not lie to you; the letter is a slap in the face. It is a slap in the face to me. It is a slap in the face to my soldiers, peers and leaders who have demonstrated that an infantry unit can be professional enough to accept diversity, to accept capable leaders, to accept skilled soldiers.

My subordinates know I'm gay. They don't care. They are professional.

Further, they are respectable infantrymen who work as a team. Many told me that they respect me even more because I trusted them enough to let them know the truth. Trust is the foundation of unit cohesion.

After I publicly announced that I am gay, I reported for training and led rifle marksmanship. I ordered hundreds of soldiers to fire live rounds and qualify on their weapons. I qualified on my own weapon. I showered after training and slept in an open bay with 40 other infantrymen. I cannot understand the claim that I "negatively affected good order and discipline in the New York Army National Guard." I refuse to accept this statement as true.

As an infantry officer, I am not accustomed to begging. But I beg you today: Do not fire me. Do not fire me because my soldiers are more than a unit or a fighting force—we are a family and we support each other. We should not learn that honesty and courage leads to punishment and insult. Their professionalism should not be rewarded with losing their leader. I understand if you must fire me, but please do not discredit and insult my soldiers for their professionalism.

When I was commissioned I was told that I serve at the pleasure of the President. I hope I have not displeased anyone by my honesty. I love my job. I want to deploy and continue to serve with the unit I respect and admire. I want to continue to serve our country because of everything it stands for.

Please do not wait to repeal Don't Ask, Don't Tell. Please do not fire me.

> *"The Army is granting a record number of 'moral waivers,' allowing even felons to enlist. Yet we turn away patriotic gay and lesbian citizens."*

DADT Causes the Loss of Valuable Personnel

Alan K. Simpson

Alan K. Simpson is a former Republican U.S. senator from Wyoming. In the following viewpoint, he argues that Don't Ask, Don't Tell (DADT) has caused the military to discharge valuable personnel, including Arabic linguists and combat engineers. Simpson notes that the public at large and the military are both much more accepting of gay service members than they were in 1993 when DADT was passed. Simpson concludes that given the serious manpower shortages in the military, DADT should be repealed.

As you read, consider the following questions:

1. What does Simpson say changed his mind about Don't Ask, Don't Tell?

2. According to General Schoomaker in December 2006, as cited by the author, what did the army have to do in order to prevent it from breaking?

Alan K. Simpson, "Bigotry That Hurts Our Military," *Washington Post*, March 14, 2007. Reproduced by permission of the author.

3. Who is Alan Turing, and why does Simpson feel his story is relevant to the discussion of Don't Ask, Don't Tell?

As a lifelong Republican who served in the Army in Germany, I believe it is critical that we review—and overturn—the ban on gay service in the military. I voted for "don't ask, don't tell."[1] But much has changed since 1993.

My thinking shifted when I read that the military was firing translators because they are gay. According to the Government Accountability Office, more than 300 language experts have been fired under "don't ask, don't tell," including more than 50 who are fluent in Arabic. This when even Secretary of State Condoleezza Rice [in 2007] acknowledged the nation's "foreign language deficit" and how much our government needs Farsi and Arabic speakers. Is there a "straight" way to translate Arabic? Is there a "gay" Farsi? My God, we'd better start talking sense before it is too late. We need every ablebodied, smart patriot to help us win this war.

In today's perilous global security situation, the real question is whether allowing homosexuals to serve openly would enhance or degrade our readiness. The best way to answer this is to reconsider the original points of opposition to open service.

First, America's views on homosexuals serving openly in the military have changed dramatically. The percentage of Americans in favor has grown from 57 percent in 1993 to a whopping 91 percent of 18- to 29-year-olds surveyed in a Gallup poll in 2003.

Military attitudes have also shifted. Fully three-quarters of 500 vets returning from Iraq and Afghanistan said in a December [2006] Zogby poll that they were comfortable

1. "Don't Ask, Don't Tell," or DADT, is the policy that prevents openly gay men and women from serving in the military.

interacting with gay people. Also [in 2006], a Zogby poll showed that a majority of service members who knew a gay member in their unit said the person's presence had no negative impact on the unit or personal morale. Senior leaders such as retired Gen. John Shalikashvili and Lt. Gen. Daniel Christman, a former West Point superintendent, are calling for a second look.

Second, 24 nations, including 12 in Operation Enduring Freedom [the war in Afghanistan] and nine in Operation Iraqi Freedom [the war in Iraq], permit open service. Despite controversy surrounding the policy change, it has had no negative impact on morale, cohesion, readiness or recruitment. Our allies did not display such acceptance back when we voted on "don't ask, don't tell," but we should consider their common-sense example.

More Troops Are Needed

Third, there are not enough troops to perform the required mission. The Army is "about broken," in the words of [former chairman of the Joint Chiefs of Staff and former secretary of state] Colin Powell. The Army's chief of staff, Gen. Peter Schoomaker, told the House Armed Services Committee in December [2006] that "the active-duty Army of 507,000 will break unless the force is expanded by 7,000 more soldiers a year." To fill its needs, the Army is granting a record number of "moral waivers," allowing even felons to enlist. Yet we turn away patriotic gay and lesbian citizens.

The Urban Institute estimates that 65,000 gays are serving and that there are 1 million gay veterans. These gay vets include Capt. Cholene Espinoza, a former U-2 pilot who logged more than 200 combat hours over Iraq, and Marine Staff Sgt. Eric Alva, who lost his right leg to an Iraqi land mine. Since 2005, more than 800 personnel have been discharged from "critical fields"—jobs considered essential but difficult in terms of training or retraining, such as linguists, medical personnel

Public Attitudes Toward Gays in the Military Depends on How the Question Is Phrased

Do You Favor or Oppose _____ *Serving in the Military?*

	"Homosexuals"	"Gay Men & Lesbians"
Strongly Favor	34%	51%
Somewhat Favor	25%	19%
Somewhat Oppose	10%	7%
Strongly Oppose	19%	12%

TAKEN FROM: Kevin Hechtkopf, "Support for Gays in the Military Depends on the Question," *CBS News Online*, February 11, 2010. www .cbsnews.com.

and combat engineers. Aside from allowing us to recruit and retain more personnel, permitting gays to serve openly would enhance the quality of the armed forces.

In World War II, a British mathematician named Alan Turing led the effort to crack the Nazis' communication code. He mastered the complex German enciphering machine, helping to save the world, and his work laid the basis for modern computer science. Does it matter that Turing was gay? This week [in March 2007], Gen. Peter Pace, chairman of the Joint Chiefs, said that homosexuality is "immoral" and that the ban on open service should therefore not be changed. Would Pace call Turing "immoral"?

Since 1993, I have had the rich satisfaction of knowing and working with many openly gay and lesbian Americans, and I have come to realize that "gay" is an artificial category when it comes to measuring a man or woman's on-the-job performance or commitment to shared goals. It says little about the person. Our differences and prejudices pale next to our historic challenge. Gen. Pace is entitled, like anyone, to his personal opinion, even if it is completely out of the mainstream of American thinking. But he should know better than to assert this opinion as the basis for policy of a military that represents and serves an entire nation. Let us end "don't ask, don't tell." This policy has become a serious detriment to the readiness of America's forces as they attempt to accomplish what is arguably the most challenging mission in our long and cherished history.

> *"The prohibition against open service by homosexuals is not an anti-gay measure. It's a common sense policy."*

Keeping Gays Out of the Military Does Not Cause Serious Personnel Loss

Larry Thornberry

Larry Thornberry is a writer living in Tampa, Florida, and is a contributor to the American Spectator. *In the following viewpoint, he argues that America should not allow gays and lesbians to openly serve in the military. Thornberry contends that Don't Ask, Don't Tell (DADT) needs to go further and prevent open homosexuals from joining the military instead of simply allowing them to serve quietly. He believes that a strong American military could be maintained better without having to deal with tension and resentments that would result from having gays in the barracks.*

As you read, consider the following questions:

1. Why does the author state that we should not "be impressed with the news that Canada allows homosexuals to serve openly"?

Larry Thornberry, "The Wrong Gay Line," *The American Spectator*, February 8, 2010. Reproduced by permission.

2. According to the article, what percentage of the military force is straight?

3. Instead of focusing on getting gays into the military, where does Thornberry say the civilian and military leadership should redirect their energy?

Wilford Brimley, the folksy and appealing character actor, did a series of commercials a few years back for a brand of oatmeal, the signature line of which was, "It's the right thing to do."

I don't know if eating oatmeal is the right thing to do; it's certainly an uninteresting thing to do. But I know Admiral Michael Mullen, chairman of the Joint Chiefs of Staff, is wrong when he claims that allowing openly homosexual men and women to serve in the U.S. military is "the right thing to do."

Allowing Gays in Military Would Make It Less Effective

Putting gays and lesbians in the barracks and ships' sleeping compartments, not to mention those communal showers, would be an extraordinarily disruptive thing to do. It would make our military less effective. It would hurt recruiting. It would be a thumb in the eye of the men and women of our military who've been performing well and bravely under very tough conditions.

We've had endless evidence that our rookie president doesn't know or care about any of these things. So it's no surprise that he would put left social engineering ahead of national security (about which he is clueless). But it's more than a little disappointing to learn that the Chairman of the Joint Chiefs doesn't either. Even our Secretary of Defense has chosen politics over security.

I'm really surprised at how many people, including journalists who should know better, claim to be surprised that the admiral buckled on this one. Mullen may or may not have been a warrior earlier in his naval career. But he's a courtier now, and he must say what the court wants to hear. Or at least he thinks he does.

"Who would have thought that the most emphatic statement in favor of gay rights would come from a military leader—instead of a court, a state legislature, or a popular vote?" the lead to an editorial in the *Greenwood Commonwealth* of Greenwood, Mississippi asks.

Well, just about anyone familiar with the military officer promotion system at the highest levels would not be surprised by this sort of toadying. Sadly, after about lieutenant colonel in the Army, Air Force, and Marine Corps, and commander in the Navy, promotion gets very political. Too often the warriors get left behind while bureaucrats and politicians are lifted up.

Civilian control of the military does not require top military officers to roll over for policies that make it harder for our military to accomplish the tough missions we give it (not to mention the crack-pot social-work deployments we shouldn't be giving it). But too often that's just what we get. General Patsy Schroeder comes up with yet another daft idea and the guys with the stars on their shoulder-boards salute and ask, "How high?"

The debate on this issue threatens to establish a new NCAA record for non-sequiturs. One of the non-sequiturs supporters of this policy trot out is that gays have always served secretly but honorably, often bravely, in the military. True, but irrelevant. As is the assertion that public support for gay people has increased, which it clearly has. And don't be impressed with the news that Canada allows homosexuals to serve openly and that this, pro-gay-service types say, causes no problem. Canada's military is about the size of the Tampa Police Department and may have even less firepower.

Gays Not Obliged to Say Anything

Even more beside the point was Mullen's statement to Congress: "No matter how I look at this issue, I cannot escape be-

Discharges for Homosexuality Are a Small Fraction of Discharges, 2008

Reason	Discharges FY 2008	Per Day
Drugs	5627	15.4
Serious Offenses	3817	10.4
Weight Standards	4555	12.5
Pregnancy	2353	6.4
Parenthood	2574	7.0
Homosexuality	634	1.7
	19560	

TAKEN FROM: Center for Military Readiness, "False 'National Security' Argument for Gays in the Military," October 2009. www.cmrlink.org.

ing troubled by the fact that we have in place a policy which forces young men and women to lie about who they are in order to defend their fellow citizens."

Huh? No, Admiral. Gay people are not obliged to lie. Under the current policy they're not obliged to say anything. They simply have to face the fact that their open presence in the close quarters of military life just won't do. No shame in it. The prohibition against open service by homosexuals is *not* an anti-gay measure. It's a common sense policy.

The overwhelming and obvious reason why openly homosexual men and women should not be allowed to serve is the imposition this would pose on straights in uniform, which will always be 95+ percent of the force, even if openly gay people are allowed in.

As the draft ended in 1973, fewer and fewer Americans, including journalists and politicians who whoop up this insane idea, have had military experience. So they have no understanding of the close, intimate quarters soldiers, sailors, Marines, and airmen, particularly the lower enlisted ranks, live in.

Close Quarters

Military life is not like civilian life. During operations it's not a 9-5 job where people go home at night to the privacy of their own homes. The last thing straight service members need is the sexual tension caused by having gays and lesbians showering and sleeping just feet away from them. When I was an enlisted destroyer sailor, under a no-gays-even-in-the-closet policy, I had the comfort of knowing that anyone in the open showers I had to share with my shipmates was only there for the purpose of getting clean.

If we're going to throw gay and straight servicemen into the same open showers together, we may as well go the rest of the way and throw servicemen and women in together. What's the difference? Or are we going to have new combinations and permutations of facilities—his, hers, theirs, and niche?

You don't have to be anti-gay to not want to be involved in intimate functions with members of your own sex who might consider you a sex object. This policy would hurt recruitment at a time when America is involved in two wars and the military is having a difficult enough time keeping the ranks filled. People who serve in the military know this, even high-ranking officers (and when they're off the record they'll say it). So does Mullen when he's not concentrating on how to cater to his civilian political bosses. Or has he been away from service on warships and in the Pentagon so long he's forgotten?

This issue may instruct us on whether the Republican Party has learned anything about standing for something rather than falling for anything. To the usual suspects on the cultural left the military is just a huge, expensive ball of clay to be molded to their liking. They'll push for a gay-friendly military using the tired and irrelevant charges of discrimination and homophobia. This nonsense should be resisted, even though the left, with full support from the left-stream media, will go full-goose hysterical and call anyone who opposes this lark a hater.

A strong military is good for America. A militarily strong America is good for the world. We can maintain that strength better without having to sort out and deal with all the various tensions, resentments, and counter-resentments that would be the inevitable result of gays in the barracks. Americans would be thankful if our leadership, civilian and military, would redirect the energy they're now wasting trying to get gays into the military toward keeping Muslim jihadists out of it.

> "I feared that reporting the abuse would lead to an investigation into my sexuality."

DADT Worsens Harassment of Gay Men in the Military

Joseph Christopher Rocha

Joseph Christopher Rocha is a former U.S. Navy petty officer third class. In the following viewpoint taken from an open letter to President Barack Obama, he explains that he joined the navy out of a desire to serve and kept his sexual orientation secret; however, others in his unit decided he was homosexual and abused him. Because of "Don't Ask, Don't Tell," he was unable to report the abuse. Eventually, despite being accepted for officer training, he decided that he could not continue to serve dishonestly. In light of his experiences, he urges President Obama to repeal "Don't Ask, Don't Tell" so that openly gay men and women can serve without dishonesty or fear of harassment.

As you read, consider the following questions:

1. Why does Rocha say that his comrades decided he was homosexual?

Joseph Christopher Rocha, "Stories from the Frontline: Former Navy Petty Officer Third Class, Joseph Rocha," Servicemembers Legal Defense Network, May 3, 2010. Reproduced by permission.

2. The author says he is not angry about his abuse, but about what?

3. What does Rocha say he would forfeit by continuing to serve under DADT?

Dear Mr. President,

After the recent letter by Secretary of Defense Robert Gates recommended the repeal of "Don't Ask, Don't Tell" [the policy that prevents openly gay servicemembers from serving in the military] be delayed, this is my plea to you on the behalf of the soldiers serving in silence to end this law now:

I never wanted anything more in my life than to be a career officer. My entire childhood I was exposed to abuse, violence, and crime. I came out of it all with a simple, yet overwhelming desire to serve. When my first attempt at getting into the Naval Academy failed, I waited restlessly until I turned eighteen. I enlisted on my birthday and set off to prove myself to the Academy. I was eager to leave the cruelty of my past and join a true family.

I knew I was gay, but it was irrelevant to me then. I was determined to join an elite team of handlers working with dogs trained to detect explosives. As I studied hard to pass exams and complete training, I was convinced that the current law would protect me. I knew that based on merit and achievement I would excel in the military.

I never told anyone I was gay. But a year and a half later while serving in the Middle East, I was tormented by my chief and fellow sailors, physically and emotionally, as they had their suspicions. The irony of "Don't Ask, Don't Tell" [DADT] is that it protects bigots and punishes gays who comply.

Shop talk in the unit revolved around sex, either the prostitute-filled parties of days past or the escapades my comrades looked forward to. They interpreted my silence and total

DADT Enables Discrimination

By establishing special rules for gays and lesbians that do not apply to heterosexuals, the "don't ask, don't tell" policy codified anti-homosexual discrimination. By stigmatizing homosexuality, the policy has also perpetuated prejudice against and invited harassment of gay servicemembers. In theory, all servicemembers are to be treated with dignity and respect regardless of sexual orientation. In practice, gay servicemembers endure anti-gay remarks, name-calling, threats, and even physical attacks.

Human Rights Watch, January 5, 2003.

lack of interest as an admission of homosexuality. My higher-ups seemed to think that gave them the right to bind me to chairs, ridicule me, hose me down and lock me in a feces-filled dog kennel.

On one day in the Middle East, I was ordered by a superior to get down on my hands and knees and simulate oral sex on a person working in the kennel. We were supposed to pretend that we were in our bedroom and that the dogs were catching us in the act. Over and over, with each of the dogs in our unit, I was forced to endure this scenario.

I told no one about what I was living through. I feared that reporting the abuse would lead to an investigation into my sexuality. Frankly, as we continue to delay the repeal of this horrible law, I can't help but wonder how many people find themselves in similar, despicable situations and remain silent. My anger today doesn't come from the abuse, but rather from the inhumanity of a standing law that allowed for it.

DADT Violates Human Rights

Three and a half years later when the Navy started investigating claims of hazing, I had finally earned my place at the Naval Academy Preparatory School [NAPS]. But instead of celebration, I began to question the life of persecution, degradation, and dishonor DADT had forced on me. I questioned the institution—our great military—that would condone and endorse this kind of treatment of its own members. The only thing I had ever done wrong was to want the same thing my straight counterparts wanted: a brotherhood and something to stand for.

At NAPS I realized that a career of service under DADT would be a forfeiture of my basic human rights. It would be a forfeiture of basic job security, peace of mind, and meaningful relationships, particularly with my fellow straight service members whom I was forced to deceive and betray.

After completing a six-week officer candidate boot camp, my commanders said they wanted to offer me a leadership role. But after what happened in the Middle East and even the suicide of my close friend, I was mentally and emotionally depleted. And so—with my knees buckling—I offered my statement of resignation in writing:

"I am a homosexual. I deeply regret that my personal feelings are not compatible with Naval regulations or policy. I am proud of my service and had hoped I would be able to serve the Navy and the country for my entire career. However, the principles of honor, courage and commitment mean I must be honest with myself, courageous in my beliefs, and committed in my action. I understand that this statement will be used to end my Naval career."

They say some people are just born designed for military service. It's the way we are wired, and the only thing that makes us happy. For too many of us, it's the only family we ever had. I am sure now, more than ever, after all the loss and hardship under DADT, that all I want to do is serve as a career military officer.

Mr. President, any delay in repeal is a clear signal to our troops that their gay brothers and sisters in arms are not equal to them. I plead that you take the lead—fight for repeal—and allow qualified men and women to serve their country.

> "Women are disproportionately pun-
> ished under the military's fingers-
> in-your-ears policy toward homo-
> sexuals."

DADT Worsens Harassment of Lesbians in the Military

Kate Harding

Kate Harding is a writer and blogger who contributes to Salon *magazine. In the following viewpoint, she reports on Private Bethany Smith, a lesbian soldier who fled to Canada seeking asylum after receiving threats from soldiers in her unit. Harding argues that Smith's predicament is typical of gay and lesbian soldiers who face harassment and abuse from their fellow soldiers but cannot speak out because of the "Don't Ask, Don't Tell" policy. Harding also notes that gay women are especially targeted for violence.*

As you read, consider the following questions:

1. According to Harding, what happened in 2007 that led Bethany Smith to go to Canada?

Kate Harding, "Lesbian Soldier Seeks Asylum After Death Threats," Salon.com, December 7, 2009. This article first appeared in *Salon*, at http://www.salon.com. An online version remains in the *Salon* archives. Reprinted with permission.

2. According to the author, Private Smith's lawyer said Smith was not attempting to avoid going to Afghanistan, but was instead attempting to avoid what?

3. Who was Ciara Durkin, and what questions surrounded her death, according to Harding?

A couple of months after learning that she was about to be deployed to Afghanistan, Private Bethany Smith received an anonymous death threat. Smith, a 21-year-old lesbian who enlisted in the Army in 2006, was stationed at Fort Campbell, Ky., the same base where Barry Winchell was murdered in 1999 [allegedly because of his homosexuality]. Like Winchell, Smith was continuously harassed about her sexuality, "receiving hundreds of anonymous 'gay-bashing' notes," according to *Women's eNews*. She was also "grabbed, shaken and thrown on the ground by a male soldier daily." The taunts of "dyke" had started as soon as she arrived, but "the abuse worsened exponentially after a soldier spotted her holding hands with another woman at a local shopping mall." So when she got a note in 2007 that described how some of her fellow soldiers planned to steal keys to her room and beat her to death during the night, Smith fled Fort Campbell to seek asylum in Canada. "It was at that point," she says, "that I knew I was more afraid of the people who were supposed to be on my side than people we were supposed to be fighting overseas."

Friendly Fire

Although Smith's first appeal for protected status was rejected, Federal Court Justice Yves de Montigny ruled that Canada's refugee board should reconsider her case. He noted Winchell's murder, the fact that gay sex violates the military code, and "evidence that [Smith] was afraid that her superiors may have been involved in the harassment and threats targeted at her" as reasons to give her another hearing, after the original findings stated that somehow a written death threat on top of

Women Face Harassment in the Military

I have talked to more than 20 female veterans of the Iraq war in the past few months, interviewing them for up to 10 hours each for a book I am writing on the topic, and every one of them said the danger of rape by other soldiers is so widely recognized in Iraq that their officers routinely told them not to go to the latrines or showers without another woman for protection. . . .

[In 2006], Col. Janis Karpinski caused a stir by publicly reporting that in 2003, three female soldiers had died of dehydration in Iraq, which can get up to 126 degrees in the summer, because they refused to drink liquids late in the day. They were afraid of being raped by male soldiers if they walked to the latrines after dark. The Army has called her charges unsubstantiated, but Karpinski told me she sticks by them.

Helen Benedict, Salon, March 7, 2007.

regular beatings and hundreds of lesser threats did not constitute "a risk to her life or risk of cruel and unusual treatment or punishment upon return to the United States." Smith's lawyer, Jamie Liew, emphasizes that Smith is not looking to avoid going to Afghanistan, but to avoid going there with people who mean her harm. "The idea that she would be deployed with people who were giving her death threats is a problem. If people in your unit are not there to have your back, you would be killed in a war and you wouldn't even know if it was because of friendly fire or enemy fire or because of someone deliberately firing at you. . . . Her situation is unique in that way."

Don't Tell, Do Harass

It may be, in that she's the first to seek asylum because of persecution from fellow soldiers, but what drove Smith to Canada is far from unique. The Human Rights Campaign's website says in its FAQ about the "don't ask, don't tell" [DADT] policy [which prevents gays from serving openly in the military], "Although gay, lesbian and bisexual service members have been held to the 'Don't Tell' portion of the policy, reports show that the 'Don't Ask, Don't Pursue, Don't Harass' parts of the policy are often ignored. A 2000 Defense Department inspector general survey showed that 80 percent of service members had heard offensive speech, derogatory names, jokes or remarks about gays in the previous year, and that 85 percent believed such comments were tolerated. Thirty-seven percent reported that they had witnessed or experienced direct, targeted forms of harassment, including verbal and physical assaults and property damage. Overwhelmingly, service members did not report the harassment. When asked why, many cited fear of retaliation." And speaking of DADT, in October [2009], the University of California, Santa Barbara's Palm Center released data that showed, in the words of *Salon*'s Tracy Clark-Flory, "women are disproportionately punished under the military's fingers-in-your-ears policy toward homosexuals." Meanwhile, violence against female soldiers in the military is rampant, and questions often surround the deaths of gay soldiers, like Ciara Durkin, whose death was ruled a suicide by the Army, even though shortly before she died, she told her family another soldier had pulled a gun on her and asked them to investigate if anything happened to her.

Even if Smith had no evidence of specific threats to her life, it's reasonable to conclude that her being a lesbian would pose serious risks to her safety in such a hostile environment. We can hope Canada's refugee board recognizes that and allows her to stay, but until the U.S. does something to address a military climate that supports harassment and violence against female and gay soldiers, many more will remain in danger.

| "If the current law against homosexuality in the military is overturned, . . . the problem of same-sex sexual assault in the military will be greatly expanded."

Allowing Gays in the Military Will Increase Sexual Assaults

Peter Sprigg

Peter Sprigg is senior fellow for policy studies at the Family Research Council, a conservative Christian policy and lobbying organization. In the following viewpoint, he argues that statistics show that in the army gay service members are responsible for a disproportionate number of sexual assaults. He says that the number of sexual assaults will rise even more if the ban on gay men and women in the military is lifted. Therefore, he concludes, lifting the ban would cause serious problems and would reduce morale and readiness.

As you read, consider the following questions:

1. What percentage of Americans are homosexual or bisexual, and what percentage of military assault cases were homosexual in nature, according to Sprigg?

Peter Sprigg, "Homosexual Assault in the Military," Family Research Council Website, May 2010. Reproduced by permission of Family Research Council, 801 G Street, NW, Washington, DC 20001, 1-800-225-4008, www.frc.org.

2. What does the author say the law requires in terms of gay men and women serving in the military, and how does he say that the "Don't Ask, Don't Tell" policy has affected this law?

3. What possible explanations does Sprigg offer to account for the disproportionate rate of homosexual assaults in the military?

A Family Research Council [FRC] analysis of publicly available documents—the Pentagon's own report on sexual assault in the military for Fiscal Year 2009, and published decisions from military courts of appeals over the last decade and a half—have shown that there is already a significant problem of homosexual misconduct in the military. This problem can only become worse if the current law is repealed and homosexuals are openly welcomed (and even granted special protections) within the military, as homosexual activists are demanding.

Disproportionate Assaults by Gays

Homosexual activist groups themselves have admitted that *less than three percent of Americans are homosexual or bisexual.*

FRC has reviewed the "case synopses" of all 1,643 reports of sexual assault reported by the four branches of the military for Fiscal Year 2009 (October 1, 2008 through September 30, 2009). Our startling finding was that *over eight percent* (8.2%) of all military sexual assault cases were homosexual in nature. This suggests that homosexuals in the military are *about three times more likely* to commit sexual assaults than heterosexuals are, relative to their numbers.

FRC and other supporters of the current law have pointed out the risks involved in having servicemembers share living quarters, showers, and bathrooms with persons of the same sex who may be sexually attracted to them.

This concern is borne out by many of the case synopses reported by the Pentagon. *The most common type of homo-*

sexual assault is one in which the offender fondles or performs oral sex upon a sleeping victim. Assaults upon victims who are intoxicated are also common.

Advocates of open homosexuality in the military often lament the fact that several thousand members of the military have been discharged under the 1993 law since its enactment. However, what they fail to note is that many of those discharges are actually for sexual assaults.

Published decisions of military courts (available on the legal search engine Lexis) give even more detail about homosexual assaults in the military. For example:

- 36-year-old Marine Sgt. Sean D. Habian used both alcohol and homosexual pornography in the course of assaulting a 21-year-old Lance Corporal.

- Marine Sgt. Steven G. Carlson, a military police instructor, took advantage of his position to exploit his students, inviting them to social events, plying them with alcohol, and playing games like "truth or dare" to identify who might be receptive to homosexual activity. One of his victims "testified that the appellant's acts shocked him, he froze, and was scared."

- Homosexual activists are fond of saying that the military cannot afford to lose the specialized skills that some homosexual service members have—such as translators and linguists. Air Force Sgt. Eric P. Marcum was a Persian-Farsi linguist—but also was charged with forcible sodomy against a male Senior Airman who "testified that Appellant's actions made him scared, angry, and uncomfortable."

- Air Force Major Rickie J. Bellanger was charged with sexually abusing two minor boys—one of whom had begun corresponding with Maj. Bellanger when he was in the fifth grade.

The military already has a serious problem with sexual assault by homosexuals. If the current law against homosexuality in the military is overturned, *the problem of same-sex sexual assault in the military is sure to increase.*

- If the law is overturned and open homosexuals are welcomed into the military, the number of homosexuals in the armed forces can only increase—leading to a corresponding increase in same-sex sexual assaults.

- Removal of the threat of discharge from the military for homosexual conduct will reduce deterrence, likely leading to more cases of sexual assault.

- If homosexuals become a protected class within the military, victims will be afraid to report incidents of homosexual assault and commanders will be afraid to punish them, lest they be accused of "discrimination" or "homophobia."

Allowing open homosexuality in the military would do nothing to enhance the readiness or effectiveness of our armed forces. On the contrary, it would clearly damage them—in part because it would increase the *already serious problem* of homosexual assault in the military.

Increased Sexual Tension

Concerns about privacy and the dangers of injecting additional sexual tension into the military are two of the key reasons that Family Research Council and others support maintaining the current law concerning homosexuality in the military, which declares:

The presence in the armed forces of persons who demonstrate a propensity or intent to engage in homosexual acts would create an unacceptable risk to the high standards of morale, good order and discipline, and unit cohesion that are the essence of military capability.

Members of the military are regularly placed in positions of forced intimacy with their fellow servicemembers—showering and sleeping in close proximity and spending time with one another twenty-four hours a day, seven days a week. The military continues to provide separate bathroom, shower, and sleeping facilities for men and women in order to protect their privacy during these intimate activities. However, allowing homosexuals to openly serve in the military would likely result, for the first time, in heterosexuals being forced to co-habit with those who may view them as a potential sexual object.

It is almost inevitable that such conditions of forced co-habitation would result in an increase of sexual tension within the ranks, to the detriment of unit cohesion, morale, and good order and discipline. Furthermore, there is a serious risk that such tension in such intimate circumstances would lead to an increase in sexual harassment and even sexual assault.

The response of those who favor allowing open homo-sexuality in the military has largely been to dismiss these concerns. They simply deny that placing people in positions of forced intimacy with those who may view them as sexual objects will result in misconduct—or at least, they claim that the rates of such misconduct will not be disproportionate to that which already occurs among heterosexuals.

An FRC review and analysis of legal decisions and Pentagon sexual assault reports has now shown this cavalier attitude to be unfounded. All sides agree that some homosexuals are already serving in the military—largely due to the nearly universal (but false) belief that current law allows homosexuals to be in the military as long as they are not open about their sexual orientation. As is clear from the quote above, the *law* which was passed by Congress in 1993 indicates that those with "a propensity or intent to engage in homosexual acts" are *ineligible* for military service. However, the "Don't Ask Don't Tell" [DADT] *policy* which was implemented by the [Bill]

Clinton Administration [in 1993] has had the effect of allowing some homosexuals to enter the military in defiance of the intent of the law [The DADT policy restricts investigations into the sexual orientation of service members].

FRC's analysis has shown that as a result, there is *already* a significant problem of homosexual misconduct in the military. This problem can only become worse if the current law is repealed and homosexuals are openly welcomed (and even granted special protections) within the military, as homosexual activists are demanding.

High Rates of Assault

Major national surveys of sexual behavior have consistently shown that less than three percent of the American population identify themselves as homosexual or bisexual. This was acknowledged by a coalition of thirty-one leading homosexual rights groups in an amicus brief which they filed in the 2003 U.S. Supreme Court case of *Lawrence v. Texas* [which ruled that laws against homosexual activity are unconstitutional]. Their brief declared:

> The most widely accepted study of sexual practices in the United States is the National Health and Social Life Survey (NHSLS). The NHSLS found that 2.8% of the male, and 1.4% of the female, population identify themselves as gay, lesbian, or bisexual.

Of course, some people who do not self-identify as homosexual or bisexual may at times nevertheless engage in homosexual acts. On the other hand, some who do identify as homosexual or bisexual may not be sexually active for some period of time. However, if we measure homosexual conduct rather than homosexual or bisexual self-identification, the numbers remain similar. According to the same survey cited in the homosexual groups' amicus brief, only 2.7% of men and 1.3% of women reported having any same-gender sex partners in the year prior to the survey.

Therefore, if the propensity of homosexuals to engage in sexual assault is essentially the same as that of heterosexuals, we would expect the total percentage of sexual assaults that are homosexual in nature to be similar to the percentage of the population who engage in homosexual conduct in general. Of course, it is difficult to know the percentage of currently serving *military* personnel who self-identify as homosexual or bisexual or who engage in homosexual acts, both because surveys of the military are difficult to conduct and because current law would give homosexuals a strong incentive to conceal such conduct. However, given the strong terms of the law against homosexuality in the military (and even the constraints on openness of the much weaker "Don't Ask Don't Tell" *policy*), it seems logical to assume that the percentage of military personnel who are homosexual is likely to be *lower* than it is in the civilian population. It is hard to come up with even a plausible theory to suggest how it could be higher.

Nevertheless, more than eight percent of sexual assaults in the military are homosexual in nature. This is nearly three times what would be expected.

If the likelihood of homosexual assault is equal to the likelihood of homosexual conduct in the population as a whole, *we would expect less than three percent of sexual assault cases in the military to be homosexual in nature* (that is, male on male or female on female).

A Risk to Order and Discipline

This, however, is *not* what Department of Defense data reveals. FRC has reviewed the "case synopses" of all 1,643 reports of sexual assault reported by the four branches of the military for Fiscal Year 2009 (October 1, 2008 through September 30, 2009). Our startling finding was that *over eight percent* of all military sexual assault cases were homosexual in nature. This suggests that homosexuals in the military are *about three times as likely* to commit sexual assaults than heterosexuals are, relative to their numbers.

A similar figure was reported by the *New York Times* in a news article on the release of the Pentagon's sexual assault report in March [2010]—but was virtually ignored in the debate over the law on homosexuality in the military. Citing a telephone interview with Kaye Whitley, the director of the Pentagon's sexual assault prevention and response office, the *Times* reported, "Of all the assaults, . . . 7 percent were male on male." (FRC's analysis showed that 7.55% of all cases were male on male, and an additional 0.61% were female on female, adding up to a total (with rounding) of 8.2% which were homosexual in nature.)

One could offer a number of hypotheses as to the reasons for the high rates of homosexual assault. If homosexuals were three times as prevalent in the military as in the general population, then this rate of sexual assault would not be disproportionate—but as we have noted, the current law regarding homosexuality in the military makes it likely that the percentage of homosexuals in the military is *less* than in the general public, not more (in which case, the disproportionate nature of the rate of homosexual assault may be even greater—i.e., four or five times more likely, or more). It would also be theoretically possible that homosexual assaults might be more likely to be reported, while heterosexual assaults are more likely to go unreported. However, it seems more likely that the opposite would be the case—homosexual assault cases are probably *less* likely to be reported, given the stigma that a heterosexual soldier might feel about having been homosexually assaulted. Again, if homosexual report cases are *under-reported*, as seems more likely, then the actual rate of homosexual assault may be even *more* disproportionate.

Since the hypotheses above seem implausible, it is hard to escape the conclusion that, in fact, homosexual and bisexual servicemembers are, on average, more likely to engage in sexual assault than are heterosexual servicemembers. This could reflect the well-documented fact that homosexual men have far more sexual partners in general than do heterosexuals. It could reflect in some way the higher rates of domestic violence that have been documented among homosexuals. Or it could reflect the general higher rates of psychological disorders that have been identified in homosexuals. An alternative explanation would be that precisely because of the situations of forced intimacy in the military, and because servicemembers may not be as much on guard against the possibility of same-sex sexual assault, homosexuals simply have greater *opportunity* to sexually exploit others than heterosexuals do. Regardless of whether the true explanation is one of these or some combination of them, the data clearly indicated that homosexual conduct poses a uniquely elevated risk to good order, morale and discipline in the military.

Risks in Sleeping Quarters

FRC and other supporters of the current law have pointed out the risks involved in having servicemembers share living quarters with persons of the same sex who may be sexually attracted to them. This concern is borne out by many of the case synopses reported by the Pentagon. Consider the following cryptic case descriptions of on-base assaults, quoted directly from the Pentagon's report:

> "Victim #1 awoke to Subject touching his genitals."

> "Victim awoke in his rack to a hand moving up and down his leg and touching his groin area."

> "Asleep in his rack, Victim #1 felt a hand grab his genitals and Subject's wrist. Subject then fled the room. Victim #2 woke up to Subject grabbing his inner thigh area and he confronted the Subject."

> "Victim awoke in BEQ [Bachelor Enlisted Quarters] to Subject kissing his neck and trying to put his hand in his pants to touch his genitals." ...

"After a night of heavy drinking, Subject got on top of Victims #1 and #2 as they slept and kissed face, neck, and stomach before being told to stop."

"Subject groped Victim's crotch several times when helping Victim, who was intoxicated, into his bunk."

Risks in Showers

FRC and other supporters of the existing law also point out the loss of privacy involved in being forced to share facilities such as bathrooms and showers with homosexuals, and thus appearing partially or fully unclothed before people who may view them as a sexual object. There are also cases in which homosexual assaults in the military have taken place in such contexts. Note these examples (which include one of the female-on-female assaults):

"Victim and Subject were drunk at a bar in Dec. 2004. Subject grabbed Victim's p---s while in the bathroom and kissed him."

"[Female] Subject grabbed [female] Victim as she was returning from shower, threw her on the bed and fondled her."

"Victim reported being pulled from his rack by Subject #1 and #2 and taken to the shower, stripped naked with his feet bound. Subject #1 (naked) waved his genitals in the Victim's face and told Victim to s—k on it."

Many discharges of homosexuals from the military are for sexual assault—not because of arbitrary "discrimination."

Advocates of open homosexuality in the military often lament the fact that several thousand members of the military have been discharged under the 1993 law since its enactment. However, what they fail to note is that many of those discharges are actually for sexual assaults. Below are examples:

"After a night of heavy drinking with the Subject, Victim awoke believing he had been sodomized by Subject while he slept. Subject admitted he had performed oral and a—l sex on sleeping victim. Article 32 Investigating Officer recommended against referral. Subject was administratively separated for homosexual conduct with an Honorable Discharge."

"Victim, who was highly intoxicated, had fallen asleep at Subject's house when Victim awoke to being orally copulated. . . . Command advised Subject will received [sic] general discharge from USN [United States Navy] for engaging in homosexual behavior."

"Victim was sleeping and awoke to find Subject orally copulating him without Victim's consent. . . . Subject was awarded a General Discharge from the USN for Homosexual Acts."

"Victim was talking to Subject when Subject claimed the two had been 'messing around' on a previous evening, while Victim was sleeping after consuming a large amount of alcohol. Subject admitted to Victim he had performed oral sex on him. . . . Per the SJA [staff judge advocate], an Administrative Separation Board recommended the Subject receive a General Discharge from the USN for homosexual behavior."

. . .

The Problem Will Worsen

The research recounted above makes it clear—*the military already has a serious problem with sexual assault by homosexuals.* If the current law against homosexuality in the military is overturned, there is only one possible result—*the problem of same-sex sexual assault in the military will be greatly expanded.* This is predictable for three reasons:

- Despite the fact that some homosexuals have been able to enlist in the military because of the Clinton Administration's "Don't Ask Don't Tell" *policy*, both that policy and the statutory *law* against homosexuality in the military have suppressed the number of homosexuals who are in the military. If the law is overturned and open homosexuals are welcomed into the military, *the number of homosexuals in the armed forces can only increase—leading to a corresponding increase in same-sex sexual assaults.*

- In addition, the current law and policy have the effect of deterring overt homosexual behavior by those homosexuals currently in the military, because they face the possibility of discharge for engaging in homosexual conduct. While other disciplinary measures are available, *removal of the threat of discharge for homosexual conduct will reduce the effectiveness of the deterrent, likely leading to more cases of sexual assault.*

- The advocates of open homosexuality in the military seek not only to remove differential treatment of homosexuals, but also to affirmatively *protect* homosexuals against "discriminatory" treatment. While this would *reduce* the deterrent to engage in homosexual conduct (including same-sex sexual assault), it would at the same time *create* a deterrent to the reporting or punishment of such assaults. *Victims would be afraid to report such incidents and commanders would be afraid to punish them, lest they be accused of "discrimination" or "homophobia."* With a smaller percentage of such cases being reported, investigated, or punished, *it is inevitable that a larger number of such cases would occur.*

Allowing open homosexuality in the military would do nothing to enhance the readiness or effectiveness of our armed forces—which is the only thing that could justify a change in the current law. On the contrary, welcoming open homosexuality in the military would clearly *damage* the readiness and effectiveness of the force—in part because it would increase the *already serious problem* of homosexual assault in the military.

Periodical and Internet Sources Bibliography

The following articles have been selected to supplement the diverse views presented in this chapter.

Paul Benedict	"Three Reasons Gays Should Not Serve 'Openly' in the Military," *War of Words*, February 7, 2010. www.nolanchart.com.
Stephen Benjamin	"Don't Ask, Don't Translate," *New York Times*, June 8, 2007. www.nytimes.com.
Gordon Block	"Q&A: Veteran Advocates for Gays in Military," *CollegiateTimes*, April 27, 2010. www.collegiate times.com.
Elaine Donnelly	"Allowing Gays in the Military Would Be Unfair and Hurt Troop Morale," *U.S. News & World Report*, June 29, 2009. www.usnews.com.
Adam Entous	"Pentagon Makes It Harder to Expel Gays in Military," Reuters, March 25, 2010. www.reuters .com.
Jennifer Harper	"View on Gays in Military Gets Air Force Guest Uninvited," *Washington Times*, February 26, 2010. www.washingtontimes.com.
John F. McManus	"Stop the Homosexual Revolution," The John Birch Society, February 4, 2010. www.jbs.org.
Deroy Murdock	"A Few Good Men," *National Review*, November 18, 2002. http://article.nationalreview.com.
John M. Shalikasvili	"Second Thoughts on Gays in the Military," *New York Times*, January 2, 2007. www.ny times.com.
Rob Smith	"'Don't Ask, Don't Tell' Puts Lives at Risk," *Salon*, May 25, 2010. www.salon.com.

 OPPOSING
VIEWPOINTS®
SERIES

How Is the Government Handling the Issue of Gays in the Military?

Chapter Preface

In May 2010, the U.S. House of Representatives passed an amendment to a defense authorization bill that repealed "Don't Ask, Don't Tell" (DADT). Shortly thereafter, the Senate Armed Services Committee also voted to repeal DADT. The two votes meant that the repeal of DADT "is almost certain to happen," according to Paul Harris in a May 28, 2010, article in the British newspaper the *Guardian*. If and when a full vote on repeal occurs, and the bill passes, Obama could then sign the bill into law.

If Obama signs the law, DADT will not be instantly repealed, however. Instead, the law would end DADT contingent upon the completion of a Pentagon review. "It is a REPEAL with a TRIGGER mechanism. The repeal will be on the books, but policy won't change until certain thresholds are crossed. Those thresholds happen to be the same conditions that Secretary of Defense Robert Gates and Adm. Mike Mullen had already set—no impact on readiness, recruitment, effectiveness, retention, and unit cohesiveness," explained Marc Ambinder in a May 24, 2010, article in his *Atlantic Monthly* blog.

The law does not actually prevent discrimination against gays; instead it leaves decisions about allowing gays in the military up to the president. In other words, it returns the military to the state it was in before Congress passed the law banning gays in 1993. Thus, in theory a future president could theoretically ban gays again. Once gays have begun to serve openly, however, a renewed ban is "very unlikely to happen," according to Dale Carpenter in a May 24, 2010, post on The Volokh Conspiracy Web site.

The Palm Center, a supporter of ending DADT, was enthusiastic about the repeal effort, noting in a May 27, 2010, press release that "President Obama's leadership has done more for gay troops than any government in American history." The Center for Military Readiness, which opposes allowing gays to serve in the military, agreed that the law was a major step, saying that with repeal "the Obama Administration will have full power to impose the full LGBT (lesbian, gay, bisexual, transgendered) agenda on the military."

There is some possibility that the DADT repeal may not become law. Defense secretary Robert Gates said that Obama "might end up vetoing" the defense bill including repeal because it contains wasteful spending, according to a June 20, 2010, article in the *Advocate*.

The viewpoints in this chapter further debate how the government has promoted or failed to promote the repeal of "Don't Ask, Don't Tell."

Editor's Note: "Don't Ask, Don't Tell was repealed by Congressional vote in December 2010. The policy remains in effect as of January 2011 until the President, the Secretary of Defense, and the Chairman of the Joint Chiefs of Staff certify that the implementation will not harm readiness, effectiveness, or recruitment and retention; formal repeal would then begin following a 60-day waiting period."

> "I will end Don't Ask, Don't Tell. That's
> my commitment."

The President Promises Equality for Gays in the Military

Barack Obama

Barack Obama is the forty-fourth president of the United States. In the following viewpoint, he says that he is on the side of gay rights activists. He concedes that progress may seem slow but that his administration is committed to advancing gay rights. In particular, he says his administration will move forward on hate crimes legislation, on laws providing help to victims of AIDS, on marriage equality for gay people, and on repealing "Don't Ask, Don't Tell" so that gays and lesbians may serve openly in the military.

As you read, consider the following questions:

1. Who is Judy Shepard, what does Obama promise her, and why?

2. Why does the author say it is important to repeal "Don't Ask, Don't Tell"?

Barack Obama, "Remarks by the President at Human Rights Campaign Dinner," October 11, 2009.

3. Who is Jeanne Manford, and why does Obama bring her up in his discussion of gay rights?

I want to thank the Human Rights Campaign [HRC, a gay rights advocacy organization] for inviting me to speak and for the work you do every day in pursuit of equality on behalf of the millions of people in this country who work hard in their jobs and care deeply about their families—and who are gay, lesbian, bisexual, or transgender.

For nearly 30 years, you've advocated on behalf of those without a voice. That's not easy. For despite the real gains that we've made, there's still laws to change and there's still hearts to open. There are still fellow citizens, perhaps neighbors, even loved ones—good and decent people—who hold fast to outworn arguments and old attitudes; who fail to see your families like their families; who would deny you the rights most Americans take for granted. And that's painful and it's heartbreaking. And yet you continue, leading by the force of the arguments you make, and by the power of the example that you set in your own lives—as parents and friends, as PTA members and church members, as advocates and leaders in your communities. And you're making a difference.

That's the story of the movement for fairness and equality, and not just for those who are gay, but for all those in our history who've been denied the rights and responsibilities of citizenship—for all who've been told that the full blessings and opportunities of this country were closed to them. It's the story of progress sought by those with little influence or power; by men and women who brought about change through quiet, personal acts of compassion—and defiance— wherever and whenever they could.

It's the story of the Stonewall protests,[1] when a group of citizens ... with few options, and fewer supporters, stood up

---

1. On June 28, 1969, gays at the Stonewall Inn in New York City engaged in violent protests against police harassment. It is often cited as the beginning of the gay rights movement.

against discrimination and helped to inspire a movement. It's the story of an epidemic [AIDS] that decimated a community—and the gay men and women who came to support one another and save one another; who continue to fight this scourge; and who have demonstrated before the world that different kinds of families can show the same compassion in a time of need. And it's the story of the Human Rights Campaign and the fights you've fought for nearly 30 years: helping to elect candidates who share your values; standing against those who would enshrine discrimination into our Constitution; advocating on behalf of those living with HIV/AIDS; and fighting for progress in our capital and across America.

Progress Is Being Made

This story, this fight continue now. And I'm here with a simple message: I'm here with you in that fight. For even as we face extraordinary challenges as a nation, we cannot—and we will not—put aside issues of basic equality. I greatly appreciate the support I've received from many in this room. I also appreciate that many of you don't believe progress has come fast enough. I want to be honest about that, because it's important to be honest among friends.

Now, I've said this before, I'll repeat it again—it's not for me to tell you to be patient, any more than it was for others to counsel patience to African Americans petitioning for equal rights half a century ago. But I will say this: We have made progress and we will make more. And I think it's important to remember that there is not a single issue that my administration deals with on a daily basis that does not touch on the lives of the LGBT [lesbian, gay, bisexual, transgender] community. We all have a stake in reviving this economy. We all have a stake in putting people back to work. We all have a stake in improving our schools and achieving quality, affordable health care. We all have a stake in meeting the difficult challenges we face in Iraq and Afghanistan.

For while some may wish to define you solely by your sexual orientation or gender identity alone, you know—and I know—that none of us wants to be defined by just one part of what makes us whole. You're also parents worried about your children's futures. You're spouses who fear that you or the person you love will lose a job. You're workers worried about the rising cost of health insurance. You're soldiers. You are neighbors. You are friends. And, most importantly, you are Americans who care deeply about this country and its future.

So I know you want me working on jobs and the economy and all the other issues that we're dealing with. But my commitment to you is unwavering even as we wrestle with these enormous problems. And while progress may be taking longer than you'd like as a result of all that we face—and that's the truth—do not doubt the direction we are heading and the destination we will reach.

My expectation is that when you look back on these years, you will see a time in which we put a stop to discrimination against gays and lesbians—whether in the office or on the battlefield. You will see a time in which we as a nation finally recognize relationships between two men or two women as just as real and admirable as relationships between a man and a woman. You will see a nation that's valuing and cherishing these families as we build a more perfect union—a union in which gay Americans are an important part. I am committed to these goals. And my administration will continue fighting to achieve them.

Hate Crimes Legislation

And there's no more poignant or painful reminder of how important it is that we do so than the loss experienced by Dennis and Judy Shepard, whose son Matthew[2] was stolen in a terrible act of violence 11 years ago. In May [2009], I met

2. Twenty-one-year-old Matthew Shepard was tortured and murdered in 1998 because he was gay.

with Judy—who's here tonight with her husband—I met her in the Oval Office, and I promised her that we were going to pass an inclusive hate crimes bill—a bill named for her son.

This struggle has been long. Time and again we faced opposition. Time and again, the measure was defeated or delayed. But the Shepards never gave up. They turned tragedy into an unshakeable commitment. Countless activists and organizers never gave up. You held vigils, you spoke out, year after year, Congress after Congress. The House passed the bill again this week. And I can announce that after more than a decade, this bill is set to pass and I will sign it into law.

It's a testament to the decade-long struggle of Judy and Dennis, who tonight will receive a tribute named for somebody who inspired so many of us—named for Senator Ted Kennedy, who fought tirelessly for this legislation. And it's a testament to the Human Rights Campaign and those who organized and advocated. And it's a testament to Matthew and to others who've been the victims of attacks not just meant to break bones, but to break spirits—not meant just to inflict harm, but to instill fear. Together, we will have moved closer to that day when no one has to be afraid to be gay in America. When no one has to fear walking down the street holding the hand of the person they love.

But we know there's far more work to do. We're pushing hard to pass an inclusive employee non-discrimination bill. For the first time ever, an administration official testified in Congress in favor of this law. Nobody in America should be fired because they're gay, despite doing a great job and meeting their responsibilities. It's not fair. It's not right. We're going to put a stop to it. And it's for this reason that if any of my nominees are attacked not for what they believe but for who they are, I will not waver in my support, because I will not waver in my commitment to ending discrimination in all its forms.

Obama Seen as Gay Friendly

[President Barack Obama] is still seen as the most gay-friendly president in history, with the caveat that the gay community is waiting for him to live up to his promises on repealing the Defence of Marriage Act, which denies the recognition of same-sex marriage at the federal level, and the flawed "Don't Ask, Don't Tell" military restrictions, which forbid officers from inquiring about their personnel's sexual orientation, but prohibit servicemen and women from being openly gay.

Obama was the first president to mention gay rights in his election victory speech and gay men and lesbians are excited—though increasingly impatient—about the prospects for equality.

Joanna Walters, Observer *(London), May 24, 2009.*

Responding to HIV and DADT

We are reinvigorating our response to HIV/AIDS here at home and around the world. We're working closely with the Congress to renew the Ryan White program [which funds AIDS care for low-income and uninsured victims of the disease] and I look forward to signing it into law in the very near future. We are rescinding the discriminatory ban on entry to the United States based on HIV status. The regulatory process to enact this important change is already under way. And we also know that HIV/AIDS continues to be a public health threat in many communities, including right here in the District of Columbia. Jeffrey Crowley, the Director of the Office of National AIDS Policy, recently held a forum in Washington, D.C., and is holding forums across the country, to seek input as we craft a national strategy to address this crisis.

We are moving ahead on Don't Ask Don't Tell [which prevents gay people from serving openly in the military]. We should not be punishing patriotic Americans who have stepped forward to serve this country. We should be celebrating their willingness to show such courage and selflessness on behalf of their fellow citizens, especially when we're fighting two wars.

We cannot afford to cut from our ranks people with the critical skills we need to fight any more than we can afford—for our military's integrity—to force those willing to do so into careers encumbered and compromised by having to live a lie. So I'm working with the Pentagon, its leadership, and the members of the House and Senate on ending this policy. Legislation has been introduced in the House to make this happen. I will end Don't Ask, Don't Tell. That's my commitment to you.

It is no secret that issues of great concern to gays and lesbians are ones that raise a great deal of emotion in this country. And it's no secret that progress has been incredibly difficult—we can see that with the time and dedication it took to pass hate crimes legislation. But these issues also go to the heart of who we are as a people. Are we a nation that can transcend old attitudes and worn divides? Can we embrace our differences and look to the hopes and dreams that we share? Will we uphold the ideals on which this nation was founded: that all of us are equal, that all of us deserve the same opportunity to live our lives freely and pursue our chance at happiness? I believe we can; I believe we will.

And that is why . . . I support ensuring that committed gay couples have the same rights and responsibilities afforded to any married couple in this country. I believe strongly in stopping laws designed to take rights away and passing laws that extend equal rights to gay couples. I've required all agencies in the federal government to extend as many federal benefits as possible to LGBT families as the current law allows.

And I've called on Congress to repeal the so-called Defense of Marriage Act and to pass the Domestic Partners Benefits and Obligations Act. And we must all stand together against divisive and deceptive efforts to feed people's lingering fears for political and ideological gain.

Hope for the Future

For the struggle waged by the Human Rights Campaign is about more than any policy we can enshrine into law. It's about our capacity to love and commit to one another. It's about whether or not we value as a society that love and commitment. It's about our common humanity and our willingness to walk in someone else's shoes: to imagine losing a job not because of your performance at work but because of your relationship at home; to imagine worrying about a spouse in the hospital, with the added fear that you'll have to produce a legal document just to comfort the person you love—to imagine the pain of losing a partner of decades and then discovering that the law treats you like a stranger.

If we are honest with ourselves we'll admit that there are too many who do not yet know in their lives or feel in their hearts the urgency of this struggle. That's why I continue to speak about the importance of equality for LGBT families—and not just in front of gay audiences. That's why Michelle [Obama, the First Lady,] and I have invited LGBT families to the White House to participate in events like the Easter Egg Roll—because we want to send a message. And that's why it's so important that you continue to speak out, that you continue to set an example, that you continue to pressure leaders—including me—and to make the case all across America.

So, tonight I'm hopeful—because of the activism I see in this room, because of the compassion I've seen all across America, and because of the progress we have made throughout our history, including the history of the movement for LGBT equality.

Soon after the protests at Stonewall 40 years ago, the phone rang in the home of a soft-spoken elementary school teacher named Jeanne Manford. It was 1:00 in the morning, and it was the police. Now, her son, Morty, had been at the Stonewall the night of the raids. Ever since, he had felt within him a new sense of purpose. So when the officer told Jeanne that her son had been arrested, which was happening often to gay protesters, she was not entirely caught off guard. And then the officer added one more thing, "And you know, he's homosexual." Well, that police officer sure was surprised when Jeanne responded, "Yes, I know. Why are you bothering him?"

And not long after, Jeanne would be marching side-by-side with her son through the streets of New York. She carried a sign that stated her support. People cheered. Young men and women ran up to her, kissed her, and asked her to talk to their parents. And this gave Jeanne and Morty an idea.

And so, after that march on the anniversary of the Stonewall protests, amidst the violence and the vitriol of a difficult time for our nation, Jeanne and her husband Jules—two parents who loved their son deeply—formed a group to support other parents and, in turn, to support their children, as well. At the first meeting Jeanne held, in 1973, about 20 people showed up. But slowly, interest grew. Morty's life, tragically, was cut short by AIDS. But the cause endured. Today, the organization they founded [Parents, Families and Friends of Lesbian and Gays, PFLAG] for parents, families, and friends of lesbians and gays—has more than 200,000 members and supporters, and has made a difference for countless families across America. And Jeanne would later say, "I considered myself such a traditional person. I didn't even cross the street against the light. But I wasn't going to let anybody walk over Morty."

Fulfilling Promises

That's the story of America: of ordinary citizens organizing, agitating and advocating for change; of hope stronger than hate; of love more powerful than any insult or injury; of Americans fighting to build for themselves and their families a nation in which no one is a second-class citizen, in which no one is denied their basic rights, in which all of us are free to live and love as we see fit.

Tonight, somewhere in America, a young person, let's say a young man, will struggle to fall to sleep, wrestling alone with a secret he's held as long as he can remember. Soon, perhaps, he will decide it's time to let that secret out. What happens next depends on him, his family, as well as his friends and his teachers and his community. But it also depends on us—on the kind of society we engender, the kind of future we build.

I believe the future is bright for that young person. For while there will be setbacks and bumps along the road, the truth is that our common ideals are a force far stronger than any division that some might sow. These ideals, when voiced by generations of citizens, are what made it possible for me to stand here today. These ideals are what made it possible for the people in this room to live freely and openly when for most of history that would have been inconceivable. That's the promise of America, HRC. That's the promise we're called to fulfill. Day by day, law by law, changing mind by mind, that is the promise we are fulfilling.

> "Homosexuality [in the military] would not just be tolerated, but advocated and promoted. Anyone who would even whisper a criticism of it would be forced out, demoted, or tried in court for sexual harassment or even hate crimes."

The President Is Betraying the Country and the Military by Trying to Repeal DADT

David A. Noebel

David A. Noebel is president of Summit Ministries, a Christian educational ministry. In the following viewpoint, he argues that gay people are likely to be dangerous spies. He says that President Barack Obama's plan to repeal "Don't Ask, Don't Tell" will weaken the military. He adds that the military will not only tolerate, but will actively promote homosexuality in its ranks. He argues that chaplains will have their free speech rights suppressed, and that the military will become disease ridden. He concludes that the military will be destroyed if openly gay men and women are allowed to serve.

David A. Noebel, "Ready for Cross-Dressing Army Generals?" *World Net Daily*, March 12, 2010. Reproduced by permission.

As you read, consider the following questions:

1. According to Noebel, what is the homosexual practice of colonization?

2. Who is Tony Perkins, and why does the author say he was disinvited to speak at Andrews Air Force Base?

3. What diseases does Noebel say would become a problem in the army if DADT is repealed?

Over 45 years ago, I was on the lecture circuit with Frank L. Kluckhohn. He had just finished writing a book entitled "The Naked Rise of Communism" (1962). Frank was an extraordinary gentleman whose career included being a correspondent for the *New York Times*, an adviser to the secretary of defense in the [Harry S.] Truman administration (1948) and holding a position in John Foster Dulles' State Department during the [Dwight D.] Eisenhower years. This is background material to an important point I want to make about our current policies regarding gays in the military.

One of Frank's responsibilities in the Truman administration was to uncover and remove homosexuals from positions of influence in the Department of Defense for "security reasons."

Gays Are Security Risks

It turns out that nearly all the major security risks (those who betrayed the United States to the Soviet Union, Communist China, etc.) also had homosexual connections. It seems that spies and homosexuality went together like Mary and her little lamb.

This was true not only in the U.S. but also in England. For example, several members of the secret society at Cambridge University known as the "Cambridge Apostles" did in fact turn on their own country to become Soviet spies, some of whom were known to be homosexuals. This list includes Guy

Burgess, Donald MacLean, Kim Philby, Michael Straight, Anthony Blunt, Leonard Long and John Asbury, among others.

President Harry Truman is one man who condoned neither homosexual activity nor communist spies in the U.S. government! He instructed both the State Department and Defense Department to identify homosexuals in government positions and dismiss them.

This is where Frank Kluckhohn comes on the scene; this became his assignment. What I learned from him would make a great book in itself, but his death in 1970 in an auto accident makes this impossible.

The one thing I distinctly remember Frank telling me about his job is the homosexual practice of colonization. Frank explained that after he would identify one homosexual, he would merely trace the person responsible for placing him in that particular department, and before long he would discover another homosexual. It seems that homosexuals would settle into a position and then use their position to hire fellow homosexuals into the same department or even move them into a higher position until the department was completely colonized.

Under President Truman, hundreds of homosexuals were removed from government departments because of their propensity for becoming Soviet/Chinese spies and betraying their own country.

Obama Is Dangerously Pro-Homosexual

How times have changed! A recent president, Bill Clinton, and our current president, Barack Obama, are brazenly pro-homosexual and are willing to do everything in their power to sodomize the finest military in all of human history—and this not for military reasons, but for social and political reasons.

Interestingly, neither Clinton nor Obama served in the military, and Clinton somehow avoided the draft.

Obama's administration is economically, socially, and politically in the corner of [British economist] John Maynard Keynes, who was a member of the Cambridge Apostles and a flaming homosexual. His "lover" Lytton Strachey referred to him as "a liberal, a sodomite, an atheist and a statistician." Keynes himself was heavily involved with Harry Dexter White (of U.S. Treasury fame), a Soviet/Chinese spy.

Now it's 2010, and President Obama, a man steeped in radical left-wing politics and a kind of Students-for-a-Democratic-Society [a 1960s radical organization] commander in chief, wants to allow "open" homosexuals in the United States military. Open homosexuality would have to include the GLBTQ gamut—gay, lesbian, bisexual, transgender and queer. [Civil rights organizations] Lambda Legal and the ACLU [American Civil Liberties Union] will insist on it. And Sen. [Joseph] Lieberman already proposed on March 8 [2010] a bill "legalizing bisexual behavior in the U.S. Military."

Allowing "gays in the military," therefore, is misleading. Once gays are openly recruited and accepted in the military, their "cousins" will follow suit (lesbian, bisexual, transgender, transsexual, intersexual, queer, etc.). Such a scenario would even make Julius Caesar, who was bisexual, blush. Among soldiers, he was known as "every woman's husband and every man's wife".

The United States is currently involved in two wars. Is the president out to destroy our military? Can any thinking American wish to see an "open" cross-dressing homosexual Army general trying to gain the trust of his troops (or for that matter, the nation)? Have we as a nation fallen so far that we need to apologize to Sodom [a Biblical city often associated with homosexuality]?

If the military becomes colonized as the State and Defense Departments were once colonized, homosexuals will indeed end up being generals and admirals. Just imagine a quota system in place that required 10 percent of officers be homo-

"Don't Ask, Don't Tell," cartoon by Joe di Chiarro. www.CartoonStock.com.

sexual (similar to the demand that 10 percent of teachers and counselors in schools be gay to reflect the gay population—although the truth is that less than 2 percent of the population is gay).

Promoting Homosexuality

But the heartache for Christians, who believe that homosexuality is a sin, unnatural, immoral, unhealthy and an insult to the God who made us male and female, is that homosexuality will not just be tolerated in the military, but promoted at every turn. Military chaplains will be instructed to ignore Genesis 19 and Romans 1. Military officers will lose their position for speaking out against homosexuality.

If you say you don't believe it could happen, you're living in a fool's paradise. Let's not forget that Obama appointed Kevin Jennings, a flaming homosexual, as his "safe schools czar." Talk about letting the fox into the chicken coop! What Jennings is keeping kids safe from is any criticism of homosexuality in the public schools, which are literally teaching it as a safe, natural and moral lifestyle.

Citizen magazine (February 2010, p. 7) carried a story by Karen England regarding an Alameda, Calif., elementary school that was developing a kindergarten-to-5th-grade homosexual curriculum that parents would not be allowed to opt out of. This follows acceptance of the now familiar children's books "The King and King," "Heather Has Two Mommies," "Daddy's Roommate" and "Gloria Goes to Gay Pride." What is less familiar is a book of essays called "Queering Elementary Education: Advancing the Dialogue about Sexualities and Schooling," with an introduction by Jennings. If Obama and Jennings are not shy about sodomizing public education, why would they be shy about sodomizing the military?!

The problem would be 100 percent more pronounced in the military. Homosexuality would not just be tolerated, but advocated and promoted. Anyone who would even whisper a criticism of it would be forced out, demoted, or tried in court for sexual harassment or even hate crimes.

Why can't thinking people see this coming?

John R. Guardiano says in an article entitled "The Intolerance and Bigotry of Openly Gay Military Service" that "the gay lobby demands not just tolerance of lesbians and homosexuals, but explicit affirmation of the same. Consequently, the gay lobby will litigate against religious believers (Kevin Jennings hates Christians, for example) and cultural traditionalists who do not acquiesce to its agenda."

Guardiano also points out that "the litigious nature of American society almost will require that these issues be fought out in the courts, where cultural traditionalists and religious believers have very few allies."

He concludes that "as a practical matter, the hierarchical nature of the military tends to suppress free thought and intellectual dissent."

We don't really have to speculate about what this censorship will look like because it's already happening.

Two days after President Obama promised in his State of the Union address Jan. 27, 2010, to dump the "don't ask, don't tell" policy, the president of the Family Research Council, Tony Perkins (a former Marine), was disinvited to speak at a prayer luncheon at Andrews Air Force Base.

According to Guardiano, the reason for the disinvite came from the military itself—"Perkins had spoken out in support of 'don't ask, don't tell' . . . and this, he was told, made his views 'incompatible for military members [who] serve our elected officials and our commander in chief.'"

The *Washington Times* explained the situation this way: "The [Air Force] Chaplain's Office retracted Mr. Perkins' invitation after his recent public comments made many who planned to attend the event uncomfortable, the Andrews base public affairs office said in a statement issued late Thursday [February 25]."

Perkins issued the following response: "As one who took the oath to protect our freedoms, I am disappointed that I've been denied the opportunity to speak to members of the military, in a nonpolitical way, solely because I exercised my free-speech rights in a different forum. It's ironic that this blacklisting should occur because I called for the retention and enforcement of a valid federal statute. Unfortunately, this is just a precursor of things to come in a post–'don't ask, don't tell' military. This legislation would more than open the armed forces to homosexuals; it would lead to a zero-tolerance policy toward anyone who disapproves of homosexuality. Military chaplains would bear the heaviest burden. Would their sermons be censored to prevent them from preaching on biblical passages which describe homosexual conduct as a sin?"

The answer unfortunately is obvious.

Disease and Immorality

And we haven't even addressed the innumerable diseases the practice of homosexuality perpetuates. Many of them are unpronounceable (i.e., cryptosporidium, chlamydia trachomatis, giardia lamblia, isospora belli, microsporidia), but deadly just the same. AIDS, gonorrhea, syphilis and anal cancer come immediately to mind in the pronounceable category. It is said that an army's greatest enemy is disease. If this is true, how will overturning the current policy of "don't ask, don't tell" make our armed forces into healthier, better fighting units?

Nor have we yet addressed the issue of moral force. Like police officers and firefighters, those in military uniform represent a powerful moral force around the world. Americans abroad, including missionaries, would much rather be rescued by a U.S. military force than a United Nations force. Haitians who survived their massive earthquake would rather see the U.S. military on the ground than any U.N. force. We've heard stories of police officers and firefighters being forced to march in "gay" parades or lose their jobs. What's to prevent military personnel from being forced into similar situations?

I believe the commandant of the Marine Corps hit the nail on the head in his address to Congress: "My personal opinion is that unless we can strip away the emotion, the agendas, and the politics and ask whether we somehow enhance the war-fighting capabilities of the United States Marine Corps by allowing homosexuals to openly serve, then we haven't addressed this issue from the correct perspective."

I don't think the gay mafia (mostly antimilitary radical leftists who seek to use this issue to make their lifestyle respectable and salable) has yet explained fully what "open" means in this context. In fact, their sexual practices can't be discussed in the open! The Bible designates them as abominable. Any television station that dared to broadcast such perversion would lose its license for doing it! Every civilization (except Sparta, Sodom and Gomorrah) has recognized this and sought to marginalize such activity for fear of corrupting their youth and destroying the heterosexual community. Have we forgotten what happened to Socrates or most recently the failings of the clergy relating to pederasty.

What the United States armed forces are asking for is their own demise! Shame on you, [defense secretary] Robert Gates! What our nation is asking for is its own demise! Shame on you, President Barack Obama! Since Kevin "Queering Elementary Education" Jennings is already in charge of making our public schools safe for homosexuality, why not appoint another czar just like him to be in charge of making the military safe for "open" sodomy?

However, if we're really interested in the truth, a comprehensive poll conducted by the *Military Times* found that just "27 percent of military men and only 17 percent of Marines favor open homosexuality within their ranks." It's not just "religious believers and cultural traditionalists" who are opposed to open homosexuality in the military.

> *"While the political logic behind the administration's thinking [on DADT] is understandable enough, the moral logic is contemptible."*

The President's Slowness to Repeal DADT Is Contemptible

Matthew Yglesias

Matthew Yglesias is a progressive blogger and the author of Heads in the Sand: How the Republicans Screw Up Foreign Policy and Foreign Policy Screws Up the Democrats. *In the following viewpoint, he points out that Barack Obama campaigned explicitly on repealing "Don't Ask, Don't Tell." Yglesias notes that the administration has moved slowly to implement repeal because of fear of a political backlash. He argues that allowing discrimination to continue out of indifference is contemptible. He concludes that the administration should repeal the policy quickly so that the military does not lose the valuable services of any more gay service members.*

As you read, consider the following questions:

1. Who is Sandy Tsao, and what did she write to President Obama, as cited by Yglesias?

Matthew Yglesias, "Obama's 'Don't Ask, Don't Tell' Hypocrisy," thedailybeast.com, May 10, 2009. Reprinted with permission.

2. According to the author, what is Obama trying to avoid by moving slowly on the repeal of "Don't Ask, Don't Tell"?

3. When does Yglesias say would be a convenient time for the president to pick a fight with the military, and what does Yglesias conclude from this?

Back in January [2009]. Second Lieutenant Sandy Tsao, a U.S. Army officer based out of St. Louis, came out to her superiors as gay, resulting, under current policy, in a dishonorable discharge. At the same time, she wrote a letter to Barack Obama congratulating him on his election and explaining her decision and asking Obama to "help us to win the war against prejudice so that future generations will continue to work together and fight for our freedoms regardless of race, color, gender, religion, national origin, or sexual orientation."

Stalling on DADT

On the campaign trail, Obama was clearly committed to ending discrimination in the military. "We're spending large sums of money to kick highly qualified gays or lesbians out of our military," he observed, "some of whom possess specialties like Arab-language capabilities that we desperately need." Ever since the New Year, however, Obama and his team have been slow-walking the implementation of their promise. On January 14 [White House press secretary] Robert Gibbs equivocated, saying "there are many challenges facing our nation now and the president-elect is focused first and foremost on jump-starting this economy . . . so not everything will get done in the beginning, but he's committed to following through." In late March, Defense Secretary Robert Gates expressed his desire to push the issue "down the road a little bit." And in late April, the White House altered language on its Web site in a way that appeared to soften the administration's commitment to changing the policy. On May

5, Tsao got a handwritten note from Obama reiterating that he is "committed to changing our current policy." Then on May 7, Dan Choi, a National Guard officer who, ironically, is fluent in Arabic, got word that he would be dismissed from the military for being too gay.

The game being played here is easy enough to understand. Obama's decision on a variety of fronts has been guided by a clear desire to avoid some of the early missteps made by [former president] Bill Clinton. And conventional accounts of Clinton's early presidency put the way he got into an early dispute with the military brass over treatment of gay and lesbian servicemembers high on the list of missteps to be avoided.

But while the political logic behind the administration's thinking is understandable enough, the moral logic is contemptible. The dismissal of gay and lesbian soldiers was unjust when undertaken by administrations that believed in the policy. But disagreement about policy is inevitable in a democracy and sometimes injustice reigns. What we have today, however, is an absurdity—an administration that clearly does not believe in the policy, that is on record as opposing the policy, that campaigned explicitly on changing the policy, and that nevertheless declines to change the policy.

Tsao and Choi are being dismissed, in other words, not because the president of the United States feels they should be discriminated against, which would be bad enough. Instead, they're being dismissed because the president doesn't feel like doing anything about it.

Indeed, at this point sure laziness and indifference seems to be the best the defenders of "don't ask don't tell" can even come up with on their merits. "In all due respect," John McCain told George Stephanopoulos on Sunday's episode of *This Week*, "right now the military is functioning extremely well in very difficult conditions so we should leave well enough alone."

As a defense of discrimination, this is pretty weak tea. The military performed pretty damn well in World War II but that didn't stop Harry Truman from ordering the desegregation of the military in the late 1940s.

Repeal Will Never Be Convenient

The problem with the arguments for inaction isn't that they're wrong, it's that they prove too much. The military is always doing important work under difficult conditions. And the president is always dealing with a variety of hugely important issues. No day is ever going to be a convenient day for the brass to stop doing what they're doing, and start dealing with the difficulties involved in getting soldiers accustomed to serving alongside openly gay and lesbian crew members. And no day is ever going to be a convenient day for the White House political team to pick a fight with the military. But that's a reason to avoid delay, not to embrace it. The current policy is as wrong as it was during the campaign, and firing skilled and patriotic linguists is as insane today as it was during the campaign.

In his letter to Lieutenant Tsao, Obama suggested that the need for congressional approval is the source of the delay. But there's some dispute as to whether or not congressional action is needed at all. And there's no doubting that the president has the power to influence the implementation. But more to the point, the White House has much ability to influence the pace of congressional action. Legislation to end discrimination in military service has been introduced, and the president could be strongly and vocally backing it rather than using the purported need for such a bill as an excuse for delay. And ultimately delay does no one any favors. The change will have to come sooner or later. In political terms, the White House may as well act decisively, take whatever hits they're going to take, and be done with it rather than letting this fester like a sore. And substantively, if the military is going to have to adjust they may as well do it sooner rather than later rather than lose more valuable personnel.

Instead of writing more letters to patriotic men and women in uniform who are tired of living a lie, it's time for Obama to start writing letters to members of Congress urging them to change the rules.

> *"DADT is wrong and it ought to be changed. . . . But . . . other things are even more wrong, and even more in need of immediate change."*

The President's Slowness to Repeal DADT Is Understandable

Jay Bookman

Jay Bookman is a columnist and blogger at the Atlanta Journal-Constitution. *In the following viewpoint he argues that President Barack Obama faces many challenges, including health care reform and a war in Afghanistan. Bookman says that these issues are important, and that Obama is right to put off dealing with "Don't Ask, Don't Tell" (DADT) until he has dealt with such matters; however, Bookman argues that repealing DADT is a moral necessity and maintains that activists should keep pressure on Obama, especially if he fails to move on repeal as his term unfolds.*

As you read, consider the following questions:

1. How many Americans die each year because of lack of access to health care, according to Bookman?

Jay Bookman, "Obama Deserves More Time on Don't Ask, Don't Tell," blogs.ajc.com, October 19, 2009. Reproduced by permission.

2. In what document cited by the author did Martin Luther King Jr. argue that demands to correct inequality are always seen as untimely by those in power?

3. At what point does Bookman feel that the gay rights movement would have every right to feel betrayed and angry if Obama has not kept his promises on DADT?

A lot of gay Americans are upset with President [Barack] Obama for delaying action to end the Don't Ask, Don't Tell[1] policy that forces more than 600 service members a year out of the U.S. military. They are protesting and criticizing the president's inaction, and they are right to protest and to criticize. Protest and criticism are absolutely necessary to produce change from a political system that resists change.

Both Activists and Obama Are Right

Public opinion is clearly turning as well. Fairness and equality are deeply held American values that largely transcend partisan differences, and the American people on both the right and left increasingly recognize that DADT violates those values. Advocates are building support in both Congress and the military to change the policy, and that work must continue.

But let me say a difficult thing: Obama is right too. As president, he is trying to craft a wise approach to the conundrum of Afghanistan, and any policy that is less than everything the military has requested is going to require political capital to sustain. This is a potentially life-or-death issue for thousands of U.S. service members, some of them inevitably gay. U.S. fatalities in Afghanistan are already on track [in 2009] to double the previously highest year, and could very conceivably double once again next year.

Obama is also trying to pass health-insurance reform that will extend coverage to 40 or 50 million Americans without it.

1. "Don't Ask, Don't Tell" (DADT) is the policy that prevents openly gay men and women from serving in the military.

By one count, more than 40,000 Americans die each year because they lack full access to health care. Many of them are no doubt gay. In fact, given the fact that gay spouses are often precluded from employer-provided insurance, gay Americans are probably overrepresented in that population. Changing that system is critically important.

So no, good people such as Lt. Col. Victor Fehrenbach, Lt. Daniel Choi and Lt. Sandy Tsao [all discharged under DADT because of their sexual orientation] should not be forced to forfeit their careers for an outdated bigotry. They shouldn't have to wait for justice. In his "Letter from a Birmingham Jail," Dr. Martin Luther King Jr. reminded the world that demands to correct inequality and injustice are always treated as "untimely" by those who do not feel their sting.

"Frankly, I have yet to engage in a direct action campaign that was 'well timed' in the view of those who have not suffered unduly from the disease of segregation," King wrote. "For years now I have heard the word 'Wait!' It rings in the ear of every Negro with piercing familiarity. This 'Wait' has almost always meant 'Never.' We must come to see, with one of our distinguished jurists, that 'justice too long delayed is justice denied.'"

More Pressure Is Needed

DADT is wrong and it ought to be changed. It is time. Beyond its impact on individuals, it is wrong as a symbol, as one of the last governmentally mandated examples of discrimination against gay Americans.

But the sad truth is that in this complicated world, other things are even more wrong, and even more in need of immediate change.

That doesn't mean we should back off. More pressure is necessary, and I suspect Obama wants that pressure. Furthermore, if the president hasn't moved decisively to keep his promises on the issue in the next two years [by 2011], the gay rights movement and all of us who support it will have every right to feel not just disappointed but betrayed and angry.

But at this moment and under these circumstances, 10 months into this presidency, frustration that feeds a renewed sense of purpose is a wiser response.

> "The Pentagon announced that it will ease enforcement of the 'don't ask, don't tell' policy."

The Defense Department Is Moving to Change DADT Without Congressional Action

Craig Whitlock

Craig Whitlock is a staff writer for the Washington Post. *In the following viewpoint, he reports that the U.S. military is moving toward making it easier for gays to serve in the military. Specifically, the military is putting restrictions on the kind of evidence that can be used to discharge gay service members and is preventing anyone except high-ranking officers from initiating investigations into sexual orientation. The defense secretary and the chairman of the Joint Chiefs of Staff have also made it clear that they are preparing to eliminate "Don't Ask, Don't Tell" entirely.*

As you read, consider the following questions:

1. According to Whitlock, how many service members were discharged under DADT since 1993, and how many were discharged in 2009?

2. According to the author, what is one activity of the Servicemembers Legal Defense Network?

3. Who is Lt. Gen. Benjamin R. Mixon, and what did he urge service members to do, according to Whitlock?

The U.S. military moved a step closer Thursday [March 26, 2010] to allowing gay men and lesbians to serve openly in the armed forces, as the Pentagon announced that it will ease enforcement of the "don't ask, don't tell"[1] policy that has been in place [since 1993].

No Anonymous Complaints

Defense Secretary Robert M. Gates said the military will restrict the kind of evidence that can be used against gay service members. For example, investigators will generally ignore anonymous complaints and make those who file them give statements under oath. In addition, only high-ranking officers—the equivalent of a one-star general or admiral—will have the authority to open inquiries or to decide whether a discharge is warranted.

Gates said the changes, which took effect immediately, will provide "a greater measure of common sense and common decency." He said the new regulations also will apply to cases currently under review, but not to those of people who already have been discharged.

Pentagon officials said they do not know how many current cases might be affected. Overall, more than 13,000 service members have been kicked out of the military since 1993, including 428 last year [2009].

Gay rights groups welcomed the announcement, saying the policy changes will make it much harder to expel gay service members. They also said that people would be less likely

1. "Don't Ask, Don't Tell" (DADT) is the policy that prevents openly gay men and women from serving in the military. It also limits military investigation of service members' sexual identity.

to file complaints after Gates and Adm. Mike Mullen, the chairman of the Joint Chiefs of Staff, said in recent weeks that the Pentagon is preparing for the day when gays will be allowed to serve openly.

Gates and Mullen "have been very clear to folks up and down the chain of command that the focus is on ending 'don't ask, don't tell,'" said Aubrey Sarvis, executive director of the Servicemembers Legal Defense Network, which represents gays facing expulsion.

The Pentagon is moving ahead on the assumption that Congress will overturn the ban on gays serving openly, which was codified into law in 1993 after military leaders resisted attempts by President Bill Clinton to integrate gays into the armed forces. Under the law, gays are allowed to serve as long as they hide their sexual orientation and the military cannot prove they have engaged in "homosexual conduct."

Preparing to End DADT

Gates asked Pentagon lawyers last summer [2009] to review whether the Defense Department had the legal discretion to enforce "don't ask, don't tell" more loosely. The process stalled until President Obama urged Congress to repeal the law in his Jan. 27 [2010] State of the Union address.

Afterward, Gates asked his lawyers to reexamine the issue, and that culminated in Thursday's announcement.

Some gay rights advocates criticized the Pentagon and White House for not making the changes earlier. "It's clear this could have been done right after the president took office," said Richard Socarides, a Clinton White House official who served as an adviser on gay issues. "This is a terrific step in the right direction toward ending this policy, but in some ways it's tragic it's taken this long."

It is unclear when Congress might act. Opposition is strong from Republicans and some influential Democrats who say that the law is working well and that it would be a mistake to impose major social changes on the armed forces when the United States is fighting two wars.

Elaine Donnelly, president of the Center for Military Readiness, a group that opposes changing the law, said "don't ask, don't tell" is "important to protect recruiting, retention and readiness in the all-volunteer force." She accused Gates of trying to usurp Congress's authority by making the changes.

Gates has assigned Gen. Carter F. Ham, the commander of the U.S. Army Europe, and Jeh C. Johnson, the Pentagon's chief legal counsel, to come up with a plan by Dec. 1 [2010] for integrating gays into the armed services. The issues they will have to sort out include same-sex marriage and barracks co-habitation.

At the same time, Gates on Thursday urged Congress not to act too quickly by repealing "don't ask, don't tell" before Dec. 1, or by approving a moratorium on discharges—something that some advocacy groups have called for. "Doing it hastily is very risky," he said.

The issue remains sensitive among the military brass. Some generals and admirals have said they are against any changes. But few have been willing to openly contradict Mullen, the nation's highest-ranking military officer, who told the Senate in February [2010] that repealing the law would be "the right thing to do."

An exception has been Lt. Gen. Benjamin R. Mixon, the commander of the U.S. Army Pacific. In a letter this month to *Stars and Stripes*, a newspaper that covers military affairs, he said that ending "don't ask, don't tell" would be "ill-advised." He urged service members and their families to lobby their elected officials against any changes.

That last part apparently crossed the line with Mullen, who said Thursday that if officers feel so strongly that they cannot abide by policy changes, "the answer is not advocacy. It is in fact to vote with your feet."

Asked if he thought Mixon should resign, Mullen told reporters, "That's a decision that would certainly be up to him."

> *"Nobody should be surprised if there are people from [the Defense Department] up on the Hill urging Congress not to vote [to repeal DADT]."*

The Defense Department May Be Blocking Congressional Action on DADT

Kerry Eleveld

Kerry Eleveld is the Washington correspondent for the Advocate, *the longest-running gay newsmagazine in the United States. In the following viewpoint, she reports that the Defense Department is trying to slow down a Congressional vote on repeal of "Don't Ask, Don't Tell." Gay advocates are protesting the Defense Department's lobbying, and are pushing the White House to move toward ending the policy.*

As you read, consider the following questions:

1. According to Eleveld, the Defense Department wants to delay a vote on repeal of "Don't Ask, Don't Tell" until what happens?

Kerry Eleveld, "Is Defense Dept. Blocking DADT Vote?" *Advocate*, April 19, 2010. Reproduced by permission.

2. According to the author, does Aubrey Sarvis believe the White House has had a hand in trying to slow down a vote on repeal?

3. According to Sarvis, as cited by Eleveld, what is the preferred vehicle for a repeal effort?

The executive director of the lead group that lobbies for repeal of "don't ask, don't tell" sent a letter [in April 2010] to President Barack Obama urging him to "reaffirm" his commitment to end the policy and charging that administration officials have been discouraging congressional action behind the scenes.

Delaying a Vote

"I am very disturbed by multiple reports from Capitol Hill that your Congressional liaison team is urging some Members of Congress to avoid a vote on repeal this year," read the letter from Aubrey Sarvis, executive director of Servicemembers Legal Defense Network, as first reported by Ben Smith in POLITICO.

Sarvis told *The Advocate* that he has gotten reports from Capitol Hill staffers in both the Senate and House that representatives from the Department of Defense have asked them to hold off on taking a vote on the policy until a report on how to implement repeal is completed. The study, ordered by Defense Secretary Robert Gates in February [2010], is due in early December.

"The administration is saying, 'Look, the working group has its task, their work is not concluded until the end of the year, and we would prefer that this not be voted on this year,'" Sarvis said.

Asked if the directive came from officials at the White House or the Defense Department, Sarvis said, "It's the Pentagon, but the Pentagon is part of the administration."

The Department of Defense was not immediately available for comment.

Sarvis said he did not know of any White House officials who had discouraged a vote since the president made a pledge to repeal the gay ban in his State of the Union address in January.

"The president has spoken, and I think those that are closest to him have not done anything that is at odds with his word," he said.

During that speech, Obama said, "This year, I will work with Congress and our military to finally repeal the law that denies gay Americans the right to serve the country they love because of who they are."

But in March, Defense secretary Robert Gates told reporters he thought it would be "risky" to move on legislative repeal before the Pentagon's working group finishes its review.

"I do not recommend a change in the law before we have completed our study," Gates said.

Asked if the White House agreed with his time line, Gates responded, "You would have to ask them, but I would tell you that my impression is that the president is very comfortable with the process that we've laid out."

Mixed Signals

Sarvis said the secretary's comments are entirely consistent with the reports he has gotten from the Hill, which have come from House staffers who work for members with a seat on the House Armed Services Committee and Senate staffers whose senators do not sit on the Senate Armed Services Committee.

"Nobody should be surprised if there are people from DOD up on the Hill urging Congress not to vote," he said. "Gates really doesn't want a vote this year, so I think they're trying to get the word to Democrats who would be receptive to not taking the vote this year."

The challenge for pro-repeal advocates, Sarvis said, is finding a way to reconcile the president's stated goal in the State of the Union with the secretary's desire to have the remainder of 2010 to finish the study. Sarvis said his organization and other groups are working to bridge that gap. Servicemembers United, a gay veterans group floated a plan earlier this year that would legislatively lock in repeal this session but respect the implementation timetable laid out by Pentagon officials.

Since the State of the Union, White House press secretary Robert Gibbs has declined to indicate whether the president would like to see Congress vote on repeal this year.

But Sarvis said the clock is ticking, since both Armed Services Committees and even the full House might vote in the next 30–45 days on the Defense authorization bill, the preferred vehicle for a repeal measure.

"The train is leaving," Sarvis said. "We could have key votes before the Memorial Day recess."

Congressman Barney Frank of Massachusetts has also displayed a heightened sense of urgency about repeal recently and even called on the White House to "make clear that it supports legislative action this year."

But Frank said he had heard no reports of White House officials explicitly discouraging a vote on "don't ask, don't tell."

"I've never heard that," Frank said. "I've talked to both Patrick (Murphy) and Carl (Levin) who are working on it, neither one of them have said that to me." Rep. Murphy and Sen. Levin are spearheading the repeal effort in the House and Senate, respectively.

Frank also said that he has not heard from White House officials since he began prodding them to take a stand on the timing of a vote.

"I haven't talked to the White House about this," he said. "Obviously, I've been sending them public messages about how unhappy I am."

Periodical and Internet Sources Bibliography

The following articles have been selected to supplement the diverse views presented in this chapter.

Marc Ambinder	"The Night Beat: Don't Ask Anymore," *Atlantic Monthly*, May 24, 2010. www.theatlantic.com.
Peter Baker	"Is President Obama Fulfilling Clinton's Promise?" *New York Times*, April 2, 2010. www.nytimes.com.
Daily Telegraph (London)	"U.S. Congress Passes Law to Repeal 'Don't Ask, Don't Tell' Policy on Gays in Military," May 28, 2010. www.telegraph.co.uk.
Shikha Dalmia	"Obama's Betrayal on Don't Ask Don't Tell," *Reason*, June 5, 2009. http://reason.com.
Philip Elliot	"White House Backs Compromise on Gays in Military," *Salon*, May 24, 2010. www.salon.com.
Jordan Fabian	"Armed Services Chairman Opposes DADT Repeal Plan," *Hill*, May 25, 2010. http://thehill.com.
Bridgette P. LaVictoire	"We Must Wait for Don't Ask Repeal, but It Should Cost Obama and Democrats Something for Our Patience," *LezGetReal*, April 20, 2010. http://lezgetreal.com.
Laura Meckler	"Deal to End Ban on Gays in Military Takes Shape," *Wall Street Journal*, May 25, 2010. http://online.wsj.com.
Sheryl Gay Stolberg	"Deal Reached for Ending Law on Gays in Military," *New York Times*, May 24, 2010. www.nytimes.com.
Andrew Sullivan	"The Fierce Urgency of Whenever," *Daily Dish*, May 13, 2009. http://andrewsullivan.theatlantic.com.

OPPOSING
VIEWPOINTS®
SERIES

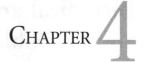

CHAPTER 4

How Do Other Countries Treat Gays in the Military?

Chapter Preface

Many nations, from Israel to Britain to South Africa to Canada, have allowed gays and lesbians to serve openly in the military. The experiences of these nations have often been referenced by commentators discussing whether the U.S. military should repeal its "Don't Ask, Don't Tell" policy.

One of the most controversial discussions around foreign militaries and gays occurred in March 2010. At a U.S. Senate hearing, General John Sheehan, a former North Atlantic Treaty Organization (NATO) commander and a senior marine officer, said that the Netherlands' military had been weakened by allowing homosexuals to serve.

Sheehan said in a March 16, 2010, article on VOANews-.com that the Netherlands "made a conscious effort to socialize their military. It included open homosexuality. That led to a force that was ill-equipped to go to war." Sheehan argued that the weakness caused by gays in the Dutch military led to the infamous Srebenica massacre of 1995. In that incident, four hundred Dutch peacekeepers, badly outnumbered by Serb forces, stood aside while the Serbians slaughtered eight thousand male Bosnian civilians. This was the largest mass murder since World War II. It led to major political repercussions in Holland, resulting in the government resigning in 2002.

The Dutch reacted with outrage at Sheehan's comments. Prime Minister Jan Peter Balkenende said Sheehan's "remarks were outrageous, wrong and beneath contempt," according to Ben Berkowitz in a May 19, 2010, article on the Reuters newswire. The head of the Dutch military union AFMP referred to Sheehan's remarks as "the ridiculous convulsion of a loner."

Sheehan had originally said he had based his remarks on a conversation with Dutch General Henk van den Breeman, the military chief of staff at the time of the Srebenica massacre.

When van den Breeman contradicted Sheehan's account, Sheehan apologized, writing, "I am sorry that my recent public recollection of those discussions of 15 years ago inaccurately reflected your thinking on some specific social issues in the military," as quoted by Mike Corder in an April 1, 2010, Associated Press article.

The viewpoints in this chapter examine the experiences of other nations that allow gays to serve openly in the military, and discuss their relevance to the U.S. debates on this issue.

Editor's Note: "Don't Ask, Don't Tell was repealed by Congressional vote in December 2010. The policy remains in effect as of January 2011 until the President, the Secretary of Defense, and the Chairman of the Joint Chiefs of Staff certify that the implementation will not harm readiness, effectiveness, or recruitment and retention; formal repeal would then begin following a 60-day waiting period."

> *"The integration of gays and lesbians ... has had little or no impact on recruitment, retention, morale, unit cohesion, or operational effectiveness."*

Australian and South African Policies Show That Gays Can Be Integrated into the Military

Nathaniel Frank

Nathaniel Frank is a senior research fellow at the Palm Center at the University of California–Santa Barbara and author of Unfriendly Fire: How the Gay Ban Undermines the Military and Weakens America. *In the following viewpoint, he reports on the result of allowing gays to serve openly in the militaries of Australia and South Africa. In Australia, he says, integration of gays has had no effect on morale, and the greater openness has even improved unit cohesion. In South Africa, Frank contends, antigay attitudes remain, but nonetheless the integration of gays has had no negative effects on morale or readiness.*

Nathaniel Frank, "Foreign Militaries 2010: A Global Primer," palmcenter.org, February 2010. Reproduced by permission of the author.

As you read, consider the following questions:

1. According to Dr. Hugh Smith, as cited by Frank, what did the lack of empirical data about integrating gays into the Australian military show?

2. What did the Returned and Services League (a veterans group) fear would happen if gays were allowed in the Australian military, and how did it change its position following the integration of gays, according to the author?

3. How are service members' attitudes toward gay commanding officers in the South African military contradictory, according to Frank?

In June 1993, seven months after the Australian ban on homosexual service was lifted, the U.S. General Accounting Office conducted interviews with ADF [Australian Defense Force] officials to document early outcomes associated with the change. The short overview of the policy change concludes with a summary statement based on comments from an Australian official who stated that, "although it is too early to assess the results of the revised policy, no reported changes have occurred in the number of persons declaring his or her sexual preference or the number of recruits being inducted. Effects on unit cohesiveness have not yet been fully determined. However, early indications are that the new policy has had little or no adverse impact."

A Non-Issue

In February 1996, the U.K. Ministry of Defence completed a report documenting the findings of its "Homosexuality Policy Assessment Team" that investigated homosexual personnel policies of a number of foreign militaries. A research team was sent to Australia to meet with representatives of the Royal Australian Air Force, Royal Australian Army, and Royal Australian Navy, as well as with Dr. Hugh Smith of the ADF

Academy, and service psychologists at ADF headquarters in Canberra. The British team reported that service staffs believed the change had not resulted in any notable problems for military functioning. Following an initial outcry, said the report, homosexuality became a "non-issue" and the difficulties of integrating open homosexuals were described as "just another legitimate management problem."

In 2000, the Palm Center reviewed all available data pertaining to the lifting of the ban in Australia. It found that the transition did not lead to "any identifiable negative effects on troop morale, combat effectiveness, recruitment and retention, or other measures of military performance." Some evidence suggested that the policy change may have contributed to improvements in productivity and working environments for service members. Key findings included the following:

- Prior to the lifting of the ban, ADF service chief argued that allowing homosexuals to serve openly would jeopardize recruitment, troop cohesion, and combat effectiveness while also spreading AIDS and encouraging predatory behavior.

- Senior officials, commanders, and military scholars within the ADF consistently appraise the lifting of the ban as a successful policy change that has contributed to greater equity and effective working relationships within the ranks.

- Senior officials, commanders and scholars report that there has been no overall pattern of disruption to the military. Recruitment and retention rates have not suffered as a result of the policy change. Some individual units have reported disruptions that were resolved successfully through normal management procedures.

- While the lifting of the ban was not immediately followed by large numbers of personnel declaring their

sexual orientation, by the late 1990s significant numbers of officers and enlisted personnel had successfully
and largely uneventfully come out to their peers.

- Gay soldiers and commanders successfully served in
  active deployments in East Timor [in Southeast Asia].
  Many of them describe good working relationships in
  an environment that emphasizes capable and competent
  job performance under uniform rules of conduct for all
  personnel.

- Complaints regarding sexual orientation issues comprise less than 5% of the total complaints received by
  the ADF of incidents of sexual harassment, bullying,
  and other forms of sexual misconduct. Of 1,400 calls
  received by an anonymous "Advice Line" maintained by
  the ADF to help personnel and commanders manage
  potential misconduct issues since this service was initi-
  ated in August 1998, 17 (1.21%) related to sexual orientation issues. To the degree that harassment issues
  continue to exist in the Australian Forces, most observers believe that problems faced by women soldiers are
  more serious than those faced by gay personnel.

Equal Treatment Improves Morale

Consulting experts in Australia offer evidence that cohesion
and morale are enhanced by the transition to equal treatment.
Australia's human rights commissioner said he believed his
country's termination of the ban had positive effects on the
military. "It's bad for morale to have your guys snooping on
others of your guys," he concluded. This conclusion is borne
out by evidence from gay service members, who reported after
the ban ended that the liberalized policy allowed them to
spend less energy monitoring what they and others said and
more focusing on their work. One Army captain, Squadron
Leader Chris Renshaw, who later became Senior Marketing

Officer for Defence Force Recruiting, said that under Australia's new policy, "you can be more honest. That's one of the key things about being in the military—honesty and integrity. Because you haven't got to worry about if someone's saying something behind your back, or is someone gossiping or something, because if they gossip, I don't care. So I'm more focused on my job, I'm more focused on what I'm achieving here, and less worried about [rumors] and what people think. In terms of productivity, I'm far more productive now. . . . Everything's out in the open, no fear, no nothing, no potential of blackmail, no security implications . . . nothing." Renshaw spoke of the positive impact of the new opportunity for casual banter, so much a part of the military bonding experience. Planning to take his male partner to the Christmas party, he told his superior as a courtesy. "He just looked at me with a bit of a pained expression and said, 'I expect you to behave.' And I just sort of looked at him and said, 'Look, knowing the other people that work on this floor and how they behave with booze, you're worried about me?'"

An enlisted member of the Royal Australian Navy echoed the importance of teasing as a form of bonding, and the positive role of joking even about sexual orientation: "I'm quite open about my sexuality. Sometimes the boys decide to give me a bit of a ding-up with a joke or something like that, but that doesn't bother me. We work really well together, and I'm sure it's the same for other gay and lesbian soldiers and sailors who are out, and they're accepted by their peers. O.K.—they're the object of ridicule sometimes, but everybody is." Military experts must surely understand how central it is for young people in the armed forces to navigate their relationships, in part, through playful insults and one-upmanship, at times becoming caustic or even aggressive. It's no secret that the military functions as a proving ground, both as part of the training process and apart from it. Yet many of these experts have cherry-picked instances of gay-straight tension and cast them as dangerous examples of social strife, when in fact it is part and parcel of the military bonding experience.

The director of the ADF's Defence Equity Organisation, Bronwen Grey, reported that despite early fears of deleterious consequences, the lifting of the gay ban had no adverse effects on the capability or functioning of the Defence Forces. Following implementation, she said, "Nothing happened. I mean, people were expecting the sky to fall, and it didn't. Now, a number of gay people probably didn't come out at that point, but we've had an X.O. [executive officer, the second-in-command] of a ship come out and say to the ship's company, 'I'm gay,' and, quite frankly, no one cared. There was no increase in complaints about gay people or by gay people. There was no known increase in fights, on a ship, or in Army units" and the "recruitment figures didn't alter." She said that Commanders "were watching out for problems" but "they didn't identify any. Now that doesn't mean there weren't any, but they didn't identify any." Grey summed up the transition this way: "All I can say is, from the organizational point of view, while we were waiting for problems, nothing happened. There were no increased complaints or recruiting [problems] at all. I mean nothing happened. And it's very hard to document nothing." An openly gay squadron leader, Michael Seah, said that he served actively in what is widely considered to be one of Australia's most successful military deployments in recent years—the United Nations peacekeeping operation in East Timor [1999–2005, in response to an invasion by Indonesia]. Another gay soldier commented, "Looking at the current operation in East Timor, I've got a number of gay and lesbian friends in an operational situation. I have served in Bougainville [a Pacific island once governed by Australia that fought for independence from Papua New Guinea in the 1990s], and there is no problem."

List of Foreign Militaries that Allow Openly Gay Service

1. Australia	10. Germany	18. Norway
2. Austria	11. Ireland	19. Slovenia
3. Belgium	12. Israel	20. South Africa
4. Canada	13. Italy	21. Spain
5. Czech Republic	14. Lithuania	22. Sweden
6. Denmark	15. Luxembourg	23. Switzerland
7. Estonia	16. Netherlands	24. United Kingdom
8. Finland	17. New Zealand	25. Uruguay
9. France		

TAKEN FROM: Nathaniel Frank, "Foreign Militaries 2010: A Global Primer," *Palm Center Web site*, February 2010. www.palmcenter.org. p. 136.

No News Has Been Good News

Some indication of the success of the ADF's transition comes from an interview with Commodore R.W. Gates, a senior warfare officer with substantial command experience and widespread familiarity with deployments. At the time of the interview in 2000, Gates had been in the Royal Australian Navy for twenty-nine years, having commanded a number of frigates and served in policy positions in the personnel division at Defence Headquarters in Canberra. He was subsequently promoted to Commodore in the Joint Personnel area in Career Management Policy, and later became Director General of Career Management Policy. Like other observers, the Commodore described mixed opinions and strong emotions within the Forces at the prospect of allowing homosexuals to serve openly: while nobody would deny that homosexuals existed in the ADF, whether they should "declare" their orientation was another matter. When the policy did change, serious protests all but disappeared, and formerly closeted personnel stepped forward successfully and largely uneventfully. "I must admit," said Gates, "after it happened, it's been an absolute non-event.

We've had some major cases of people declaring. Probably the most that I recall . . . would be one of our executive officers of a destroyer, the second-in-command. He declared. And, I'll be frank, it created a bit of a stir. We're talking about a mid-rank lieutenant commander in an absolute critical position on board a major warship, one heartbeat from command. . . . That person under the new policy was certainly not removed from the ship, and in fact completed his full posting." The Commodore attributes the largely successful transition to a broader effort on the part of top officials in the Navy and the ADF to develop aggressive new training protocols to minimize harassment and maximize equality of opportunity.

Dr. Hugh Smith, a professor at the University of New South Wales and at the Australian Defence Force Academy, echoed Gates' judgment. A leading academic authority on military personnel policy, Professor Smith said that the lifting of the ban did not lead to any significant effects on military performance, combat effectiveness, or unit cohesion. Like other respondents, he characterized the outcome of the policy change as a virtual "non-issue," with little remaining salience in government, media, or military circles. The lack of quantitative empirical data regarding the policy change constituted, in his opinion, a form of evidence. In Professor Smith's words, "This is not a subject that has troubled the Defence Force to the extent that they have felt that studies have needed to be done on it. The lack of evidence is evidence." He explained that when government ordered the military to lift the ban, some officers said, "Over my dead body, if this happens I'll resign." However, Smith said that there were no departures and that the change was accepted in "true military tradition." To the degree that problems of sexual misconduct and harassment continue in the ADF, Professor Smith indicated that they are mostly related to the treatment of women in the ranks and incidents of hazing (referred to as "bastardization") in the Academy.

No Problems with Morale or AIDS

In 2000, retired Major General Peter Philips was president of the Returned and Services League (RSL) of Australia, a major veterans group similar to the American Legion. In 1993, the RSL was an ardent opponent of proposals to lift the ban, arguing that doing so would jeopardize morale, unit cohesion, performance, and decency in the Armed Forces and would hasten the spread of AIDS. Asked whether any of these problems had come to pass, he told researchers that openly gay service has "not been a significant public issue. The Defence Forces have not had a lot of difficulty in this area." Probed for evidence suggesting that allowing homosexuals to serve impaired military performance, combat effectiveness, or unit cohesion, he replied, "If the issue had arisen, it would have in [peacekeeping operations in] East Timor. I haven't heard of any gay issues in that."

Major General Philips acknowledged that some gay personnel had come out to peers but disagreed with assertions made by some groups that there were significant numbers in combat units. Journalist David Mills, who interviewed service members for several stories dealing with same-sex partner benefits and combat service in East Timor, gave a conflicting account. For his investigation of East Timor, Mr. Mills spoke with gay soldiers who had served actively. He was aware of seven or eight active duty soldiers serving in East Timor who self-identify as gay, and he interviewed an enlisted Army soldier who worked as a firefighter. In 2000 he reported, "I spoke with a guy who is serving in the Army, a six-month stint in East Timor, speaking about his experiences. He was an interesting guy who said there is a lot less homophobia in the Armed Forces than you might think, although he was pretty selective about who he was open about his sexuality with. . . . He said he didn't have any problem with [coming out] whatsoever, although there was an element of surprise when he told people."

By 2009, the RSL had withdrawn its opposition to openly gay service. Retired Major General Bill Crews, its former president, said that year that concerns about morale and AIDS had not panned out. "I was there in the early days of it," he said. "I thought there'd be a continuing problem because of prejudice that exists in parts of the community." He said, "I don't see any evidence now that homosexuals are in any way discriminated against. A homosexual can be just as effective a soldier as a heterosexual."

In the spring of 2009, 100 active-duty service members, including at least one general, marched in Sydney's Gay and Lesbian Mardi Gras Parade holding an ADF banner. Chief Petty Officer Stuart O'Brien, who has served in the navy for nearly 20 years, reported that he worked shoulder to shoulder with U.S. military personnel in Baghdad in 2006, and that being openly gay was not an issue in those or other operations. "They valued the work that I did and that's all that it comes down to at the end of the day," O'Brien told the Associated Press in 2009. "Sexuality has nothing to do with anything any more within the services."

Neil James is executive director of the Australian Defence Association, a non-partisan, independent national security think tank. He is a graduate of the Royal Military College, served in the Australian Army for more than thirty years, and is the author of numerous ADF and Army operational manuals and journal articles on the Australian military. James' 2009 assessment of the ADF policy change was that it was uneventful besides some surprising disclosures of the sexuality of high-level officers. "Everyone said, 'Good heavens, that's a bit of a surprise,' and after five minutes the conversation reverted back to football," he said. "After a while it was met with a collective yawn."

Currently the ADF recognizes a range of same-sex relationships on generally equal footing with married relationships. As of December 2005, the military agreed to grant same-sex couples in recognized "interdependent partnerships" the same rights and privileges afforded to members with other types of dependants, such as a spouse or children. To gain ADF recognition of an interdependent partnership, members must prove they maintain a common household with their partner (who may be of the same or opposite sex but is someone to whom they are not legally married), and that they have lived together on a permanent basis for at least 90 continuous days. Once a service member has proven the existence of such an interdependent partnership, the couple are entitled to receive the same benefits as legally married couples, including income support and relocation, housing, education, and/or travel assistance. Recently Australia's largest community-based LGBT [lesbian, gay, bisexual, and transgender] health organization partnered with other groups to launch "Pride in Diversity," a not-for-profit program created to assist Australian employers with the inclusion of LGBT employees. The Department of Defence joined with a number of other prestigious Australian employers, including the Australian police force, to become a foundation member of the program.

A Single Standard

In 1992 when a government committee recommended the ADF drop its gay ban, the full government voted to end the policy and Prime Minister Paul Keating ordered that the policy change be implemented immediately across all services of the ADF. In place of the previous ban, the government issued a more general instruction on "sexual misconduct policy." Among other provisions, the new instruction referred to unacceptable conduct without making a distinction between homosexuality and heterosexuality. Rather than define what was unacceptable based upon sexual orientation, the new instruction prohibited any sexual behavior that negatively impacted group cohesion or command relationships, took advantage of subordinates, or discredited the ADF, and provided commanders with latitude to judge whether a certain behavior was acceptable or not in a certain context.

Assessments by the U.S. General Accounting Office, the British Ministry of Defence, and the ADF itself all found that the change in policy has been successful and has not led to any perceptible decline in operational effectiveness, morale, unit cohesion, retention, or attrition. In fact, ADF officials and independent observers believe that changes associated with the policy have contributed to a working environment that is freer from the burdensome and unproductive consequences of mistrust, misunderstanding, and misjudgment that at times compromised the integrity of units in the past.

In the decade following the policy change, some concerns remained about uneven and partial implementation of the policy, and about isolated instances of discrimination and harassment, which also disproportionately affected heterosexual women. More recently, however, the fact that the debate over gays in the military has shifted away from the question of whether homosexual soldiers undermine military performance and toward a practice of treating all members according to a single standard also stands as a testament to the success of the inclusive policy.

The South African Experience

In 2000 the South African Department of Defence undertook a major study to fully assess the environment for gay and lesbian personnel in the military. An in-depth survey was completed by 2,648 regular force members. The survey report noted that many respondents were undecided on many survey questions, and that there was often a large disparity between the attitudes of various subgroups within the SANDF [South African National Defense Force] regarding gays and lesbians. On many issues, officers, whites, personnel from the military medical service (SAMHS), and personnel in the Office of the

Secretary for Defence held more pro-gay attitudes than Africans, members of the Army, and members with lower ranks.

Overall the results suggested that the transition had proceeded with great success despite military opinion remaining mixed. Only a quarter of the respondents agreed with the statement, "I feel good about the integration of gays in the military" while nearly a half disagreed. Just over a quarter were "undecided." The question leaves unclear whether those who did not feel good about the integration of gays were opposed to service by gays or felt the climate for gays in uniform was simply not positive. However, half of respondents agreed with the statement, "I do not mind my co-worker being a gay or a lesbian" while only a third disagreed. More respondents were opposed to having a gay commanding officer than were in support (43% to 41%) even though a larger number disagreed with the statement, "Gays and lesbians as leaders do not command the same respect and obedience from subordinates as heterosexual leaders" than agreed with it (40% to 34%). Interestingly, a plurality of respondents agreed that gays in uniform would "undermine social cohesion." Only a third thought gays and lesbians were "morally weaker" than heterosexuals, while nearly two fifths disagreed with this statement.

While these opinion polls are inconclusive, this fact in itself is illuminating, since the overall research indicates a successful transition to openly gay service. In 2003, the Palm Center conducted a study that found that the integration of gay and lesbian personnel into SANDF had been achieved without any significant impact on effectiveness. The study, based on interviews with over two dozen experts and a comprehensive review of all relevant government documents, newspaper articles, academic studies, and other materials, found the following:

- The integration of gays and lesbians in the SANDF has had little or no impact on recruitment, retention, morale, unit cohesion, or operational effectiveness.

- Some gays and lesbians who served in the apartheid [a policy which institutionalized discrimination against blacks] era military (pre-1994) were subject to aversion shock therapy, chemical castration, hormonal and drug therapy, and other forms of abuse and torture.

- While anti-gay attitudes still exist at the level of the unit and in more rural areas, there has been a steady improvement in attitudes towards gays and lesbians in the SANDF. When expressed, anti-gay sentiment has been subtle in its expression and has not involved overt acts of harassment, discrimination, or anti-gay violence.

- There is no significant public opposition to the policy of integration.

- There has been no mass coming-out as a result of the policy change, but gays and lesbians within the SANDF report an increased level of comfort and are increasingly viewing the SANDF as a career option.

- The SANDF initially included a statement of non-discrimination against sexual minorities in its policy on Equal Opportunity and Affirmative Action, but is now in the process of adopting a separate, stand-alone, and much more detailed policy on sexual orientation in the SANDF.

- The SANDF is in the process of eliminating all residual bias against sexual minorities in subsidiary policies. Same-sex "life-partners" now have equal access to health benefits.

- Racial integration occurred at the same time as the integration of the sexual minorities within the SANDF. Racial integration has been a far more difficult process than the integration of sexual minorities.

"*Gay men and women are now serving with pride and distinction alongside their heterosexual colleagues at the front line of operations worldwide.*"

Gay British Soldiers Serve Openly in the Military

Craig Jones

Craig Jones is a lieutenant commander and the head of diversity at Barclay's Wealth. In the following viewpoint, he discusses his experience with serving in the British military after the "gay ban" was lifted. Jones notes that lifting the ban allowed homosexuals to serve more openly, but that it was not welcomed by many in the British military establishment. Ultimately gay military men and women can now serve with pride alongside heterosexual colleagues and enjoy increasing levels of support.

As you read, consider the following questions:

1. As stated in the article, when did the repeal of the U.K. Armed Forces "gay ban" take place?

2. According to Jones, was he one of those who had insight or was incensed?

Craig Jones, "Gay in the Armed Forces," the *New Statesman*, July 28, 2008. Reproduced by permission.

3. Would you say Craig Jones's experience of being gay in the British military was rewarding? Why or why not?

As Geoff Hoon announced the repeal of the UK Armed Forces 'gay ban' on 13th January 2000, just a few yards down the road there were long faces in the Ministry of Defence.

The repeal of the 'gay ban' was a critically important win for equality group Stonewall and heralded the beginnings of Blairite social changes which have made the UK a far better place for gay men and women to be. But be in no doubt, it was not welcomed by many in the British military establishment.

My commanding officer told a packed Officers' Mess of the policy change a day before the House of Commons announcement and we were all placed under strict embargo. My response was swift and instinctive; I stepped from my closet and claimed the ground which had been so hard fought for.

It was a matter of duty—gay or straight a concept all servicemen and women understand. The House of Commons announcement had freed me from the necessity to guard the details of my life for fear of exposure, disgrace and dismissal.

Growing Support

Secrecy and deceit go against the grain of the often-enduring friendships that we enjoy in the Armed Forces. My ship's company seemed to recognise that my choice of openness set me on a difficult path and after a bewildering first week I felt their growing support.

I cannot think of a civilian life equivalent to the 'band of brothers' atmosphere that exists in the wardroom of a warship. And it was profoundly rewarding to see attitudes and ideas about being gay change over time.

Yet beyond the few units who won themselves an 'out' guy or girl, in Whitehall the MoD fumbled around and achieved

Allowing Gays to Serve Has Had No Ill Effects in Britain

Since it began allowing gays to serve in the armed forces in 2000, none of the British military's fears—about harassment, discord, blackmail, bullying or an erosion of unit cohesion or military effectiveness—has come to pass, according to the Ministry of Defense, current and former members of the services, and academies specializing in the military. The biggest news about the policy, they say, is that there is no news.

Sarah Lyall, "Despite Misgivings, Gays Blend In to British Military," New York Times, May 16, 2007. www.nytimes.com.

little for a number of years at substantial cost to a courageous group of junior ranks who took the difficult path of being open.

At times I have defended my kind like a tiger and as I depart the service it's timely to acknowledge that there is a group of wounded senior officers who have received acerbic letters, emails or—far worse—a visit from me over the years. The fact that I have escaped 'jankers' makes me think that they took my unmilitary directness with a pinch of 'sea salt'—a faint heart never won a fair maiden.

It's sometimes difficult to tell the difference between those who have insight and those who are simply incensed; on most occasions I feel I had a little of both. Nevertheless I suspect that admirals, generals and air marshalls have traded my letters in the gentlemen's clubs of London.

The exception was Admiral Lord West of Spithead, now minister for internal security. His unstinting early support for the gay community in the Armed Forces paved the path others would later follow when the shrapnel stopped flying. His successor Admiral Sir Jonathan Band has matched his initiative despite the occasional recalcitrance of other services.

Serving with Pride

So eight years on as the Bristish Army joins Stonewall's good employers scheme and gay sailors, soldiers and air folks march through London with swords drawn and shiny medals, clapped and cheered by an adoring crowd—has this social experiment worked? Gay men and women are now serving with pride and distinction alongside their heterosexual colleagues at the front line of operations worldwide.

They enjoy increasing levels of support from their command and service chiefs and the Armed Forces no longer dismiss highly trained and much needed personnel. A few months after Gulf War II, I chatted to a gay soldier about his experiences of being at the frontline and with a cheeky grin he lamented that his fellow infantrymen seemed 'far more interested in invading Iraq than me and my sexual orientation—but who knows they might ask me to go back and redecorate!'.

It occurred to me that I was talking to the man for whom rank outsiders had fought so hard. Gay servicemen and women of my generation will always be indebted for their courage and enduring fortitude to win equality and justice for the Armed Forces of today.

This battle for equality is as much part of the history of the Armed Forces as the many others histories which adorn the walls of the Imperial War Museum (North).

The exhibition—which runs until 12 October [2008] and is free—tells the hidden history of gay men and women in the Armed Forces through the experiences of 12 serving and retired service personnel.

> *"Israel's experience provides a relevant and encouraging lesson in what might happen if the United States lifted its ban on known gays in the services."*

Israel's Experience with Gays in the Military Could Guide U.S. Policy

Susan Taylor Martin

Susan Taylor Martin is a senior correspondent for the St. Petersburg Times, *a Florida daily newspaper. In the following viewpoint she reports that Israel's policy to allow gays in the military has been successful. There has been no impact on morale or unit cohesion, and heterosexual Israeli soldiers are broadly comfortable serving with gays and lesbians. Some U.S. commentators have pointed to the Israeli experience as evidence that allowing gays to serve openly in the U.S. military will not have adverse consequences.*

As you read, consider the following questions:

1. Who is John Shalikashvili, and how have his views on gays in the military changed since 1993, according to Martin?

2. According to the author, when did opposition to Israel's ban on gays in the military come to a head, and why?

3. What percentage of the Israeli military is gay, according to Martin?

In 1993, Congress banned known homosexuals from the military, convinced their presence could undermine morale and discipline. That year, Israel took exactly the opposite approach.

All restrictions on gay and lesbian soldiers were dropped. Homosexuals in the Israel Defense Forces [IDF] could join close-knit combat units or serve in sensitive intelligence posts. They were eligible for promotion to the highest ranks.

Fourteen years later, Israelis are convinced they made the right decision.

"It's a non-issue," said David Saranga, a former IDF officer and now Israel's consul for media and public affairs in New York. "There is not a problem with your sexual tendency. You can be a very good officer, a creative one, a brave one and be gay at the same time."

Israel is among 24 countries that permit known gays to serve in the military, and its experience is giving fodder to opponents of the United States' controversial "Don't ask, don't tell" policy [which prevents gays from serving openly in the military].

In a recent opinion piece in the *New York Times*, Gen. John Shalikashvili, former chairman of the Joint Chiefs of Staff, said that admitting gays had not hurt the IDF or any of the 23 other foreign militaries. With troops stretched thin by the wars in Iraq and Afghanistan, the United States should drop its ban on known gay service members after the new Congress has time to seriously consider the issue, Shalikashvili wrote.

The retired general's view has drawn wide attention because he supported "don't ask, don't tell" when President Clin-

Israeli Gays Have More Rights

Israel, which unarguably has one of the world's most elite and effective military operations, officially bans discrimination against gays, lesbians, bisexuals, and transgenders. Israel "has more gay rights than all of the U.S.," says Denny Meyer, a former Vietnam era Army sergeant first class who is also editor of the *Gay Military Times*. Almost 30 nations—including most countries of the European Union—have no problems with anyone's sexual orientation.

Walter Brasch, Counterpunch, *March 17–18, 2007.*
www.counterpunch.org.

ton devised it in 1993 as a compromise to the tough law Congress passed that year. Acknowledging that the issue still stirs "passionate feelings" on both sides, Shalikashvili said the debate about gays in the military "must also consider the evidence that has emerged over the last 14 years"—including that in Israel.

As a country almost continuously at war, the Jewish state has always had mandatory conscription although known homosexuals were usually discharged before 1980. The IDF's first official statement on the matter, in 1983, allowed gays to serve but banned them from intelligence and top-secret positions.

Opposition to the policy came to a head 10 years later when the chairman of the Tel Aviv University's chemistry department revealed the IDF had stripped him of his officer rank and barred him from sensitive research solely because he was gay. His testimony before a parliamentary committee created a public storm and forced the IDF to drop all restrictions on homosexuals.

No Decline in Morale

Since then, researchers have found, Israel's armed forces have seen no decline in morale, performance, readiness or cohesion.

"In this security-conscious country, where the military is considered to be essential to the continued existence of the nation, the decision to include sexual minorities has not harmed IDF effectiveness," wrote Aaron Belkin and Melissa Levitt of the University of California, Santa Barbara.

A brigadier general quoted in the pair's study said Israelis show a "great tolerance" for homosexual soldiers. One lesbian soldier said she was amazed that "people either thought my sexual orientation was cool or were indifferent to it."

The California study also cited a survey of 17 heterosexual soldiers, two of whom said they would have a problem serving under a gay commander and three expressing concern about showering with a gay colleague. None, though, objected to gay soldiers in general, and as one officer put it, "They're citizens of Israel, like you and me. The sexual orientation of the workers around me doesn't bother me."

As in the United States, though, many Israeli gays, including those in the military, are reluctant to come out of the closet until they think it is safe to do so.

"All available evidence suggests that the IDF continues to be a place where many homosexual soldiers choose not to disclose their sexual orientation," the researchers found, noting that a psychiatrist said soldiers in her care still "suspect that if they come out they won't get a good position."

Publicly, the IDF says that gay soldiers—estimated to be about 2 percent of the force—are screened the same as heterosexuals for promotions and sensitive positions. One officer said she had no problems rising through the ranks as an open lesbian.

Despite obvious differences between the two countries, Israel's experience provides a relevant and encouraging lesson in what might happen if the United States lifted its ban on known gays in the services, the California researchers concluded. Not everyone agrees.

Elaine Donnelly, president of the Michigan-based Center for Military Readiness, notes that American troops, unlike Israelis, are often deployed for long periods thousands of miles from home.

"People who live in conditions of forced intimacy should not have to expose themselves to persons who might be sexually attracted to them," Donnelly said. "We respect that desire for human modesty and we respect the power of human sexuality."

However, a recent poll of U.S. soldiers who served in Iraq and Afghanistan found that 75 percent said they would feel comfortable serving with gays. Of those who knew they had a gay colleague, two-thirds said it had no impact on their unit or personal morale.

Americans in general are far more amenable to gays in the military since "don't ask, don't tell" was adopted in 1993. Polls in the last few years have shown at least 58 percent and as much as 70 percent favor repealing the ban on known homosexuals.

"Of the minority of the public that still support the policy, that support is not about anything other than simple moral discomfort," said Belkin, director of Santa Barbara's Michael D. Palm Center for the Study of Sexual Minorities in the Military.

"It's really about morality and religion and politics, and it's not about what's good for the military at this point."

> *"The same kinds of rhetoric we heard here (in the U.S.) . . . that the military would suffer and that it's too big a risk . . . were also heard in Canada."*

Canada's Experience with Gays in the Military Could Guide U.S. Policy

Tobi Cohen

Tobi Cohen is a Canadian journalist. In the following viewpoint, she reports that since allowing gays into the military by court order in 1992, Canada has experienced no problems with morale or unit cohesion. Gay service members report few problems with advancement or harassment. According to researchers, the Canadian experience suggests that repealing "Don't Ask, Don't Tell" will not have negative consequences for the U.S. military.

As you read, consider the following questions:

1. What is the Canadian military's attitude toward same-sex marriages and gay pride festivals, according to Cohen?

2. Who is Michelle Douglas, and how was she influential in the debate about gays in the military in Canada?

Tobi Cohen, "Canada Quietly Marks Anniversary for Gays in Military While U.S. Debate Rages," *Coast Reporter*, October 24, 2009. Reproduced by permission.

3. According to Nathaniel Frank, as cited by Cohen, what kind of opposition was there among the military and public to allowing gays in the military before the ban was lifted?

While [U.S. president] Barack Obama plunges his country into a controversial debate about gays in the U.S. military, he could perhaps find comfort in the Canadian experience which celebrates an anniversary milestone next week [October 2009].

The U.S. president has promised to repeal America's policy of, 'Don't ask, don't tell' [which prevents openly gay men and women from serving in the military], reviving a heated debate in his country that has not made a ripple in Canada since Oct. 27, 1992.

Canadian Courts Ended Ban

On that day Canada's Federal Court ruled that barring homosexuals from military service violated the Charter of Rights and Freedoms in a landmark verdict that prompted more openly gay men and women to join the ranks of the Army, Air Force and Navy.

In the last 17 years, many have risen to the top in their respective fields—an otherwise impossible feat under rules that once barred the promotion of enlisted individuals who'd been outed.

Luc Cassivi is one of them.

He certainly didn't talk about his sexual orientation when he joined the Canadian Navy in 1983. He's now the highest-ranking sailor aboard HMCS *Ville de Quebec*, a commander in the Navy, and he's no longer shy about who he is.

"I've been openly gay for a number of years. My friends and my co-workers know it and it surely has not been an impediment for me progressing," Cassivi said in an interview aboard his Halifax-based frigate.

Canada's Military Is Stronger

Our view is that we are stronger together by having a very inclusive military. By allowing men and women in uniform of any sexual orientation to be part of Canada's military, the same men and women in uniform who die for the nation, Canada's military is stronger and more unified, a fighting force that is grounded in the views as a sense of duty, a sense of fairness, and inclusiveness, something which our Canadian military is happy and proud to export around the world.

The Brookings Institution, "Lessons Learned from the Service of Gays and Lesbians in Allied Militaries," May 19, 2010. p. 9. http://www.brookings.edu/~/media/ Files/events/2010/0519_military_service/20100519_military_ service.pdf.

"I'm not saying that things have always been rosy. There were periods when things were difficult for a lot of people. . . . But I think we're well past that at this point."

According to the Palm Centre, a California-based think tank focused on research related to gender, sexuality and the military, Canada is a leader among the 25 countries that now permit military service by openly gay people.

Canadian Forces chaplains have been blessing same-sex weddings on military bases since 2005 and, [since then], military recruiters have participated in gay-pride festivals in Toronto, Hamilton, Montreal and Vancouver.

Cassivi spent 15 years in tight quarters as a submariner. He said he's experienced his share of awkward moments and uncomfortable jokes. There were even times he considered leaving the military.

Performance Determines Success

But once the rules changed, he says, so did the culture. Opportunities began to surface. These days, Cassivi says, success is dictated by performance.

"It's not colour, cultural background, gender or the like. It's (whether) you are competent at what you do," he said. "If you're competent at what you do, then the team will take you in and fully integrate you."

Cassivi said coming out with his colleagues merely simplified his life. He doesn't see himself as a champion for gay rights and says this is the first time he's ever spoken in the media about his sexuality. What he's most concerned about, he says, is getting the best out of his crew.

"I believe in the power of the people who work for me. It's really about them at the end of the day," he said.

"I try to do the best job I can and if somebody sees me as a role model, good for them. If what I do inspires them to carry on and achieve their full potential, that's great, but that's for them to judge, not me."

Michelle Douglas is heartened to learn just how much things have changed for her fellow homosexuals.

The 45-year-old public servant was inadvertently thrust into the spotlight when she was discharged from the military police in 1989 because she was—in their words—"not advantageously employable due to homosexuality."

She had no idea at the time the historic impact her legal challenge would have, but as the anniversary of that fateful victory approaches, Douglas said she's thrilled to have played a "small part" in the rights movement.

"It was a real turning point for equality rights for gay and lesbian people in Canada," she said.

"To have such an institution as the military now be open to gay and lesbian service members was an important victory."

While she never did return to the Canadian Forces, she was pleased to see service members marching for the first time at Toronto's pride festival in 2008.

"I approached them and told them who I was. They kind of had heard of my case but for them it was really something they saw as history," she said.

"It was heartwarming to me to know that there had been such advances . . . that it could now be viewed as history and people could just get on with their lives and serve their country proudly and openly."

Harassment Is Rare

Megan MacLean, a spokeswoman for Canada's Department of National Defence, said the military keeps no statistics regarding homosexual members but says gay, lesbian, bisexual and transgendered people serve in all three branches of the military.

Since the rules changed in 1992, she said, incidents of discrimination and harassment have been "extremely rare."

She touted Canada as a global leader when it comes to inclusiveness. She noted, however, that the Obama administration had not sought any Canadian advice on how to tackle the thorny subject.

Nathaniel Frank, a senior researcher in the U.S. with the Palm Centre, said that's not an unlikely proposition.

Every time the debate surfaces in the U.S., he said officials look to more liberal countries like Canada and Britain. While American conservatives often dismiss Canada and Western Europe as too laissez-faire, Frank said that's inaccurate.

There was actually plenty of political opposition before the Canadian ban was lifted, he said, and a majority of male soldiers polled prior to 1992 said they'd refuse to shower, undress, or sleep in the same room as a gay comrade.

"The same kinds of rhetoric we heard here (in the U.S.) during our debate in the early 1990s and since—that this would never work, that it would undermine morale and cohesion, that the military would suffer and that it's too big a risk—were also heard in Canada," Frank said.

But a 2000 study of the Canadian experience by the University of California research group found no basis for the allegations.

Lesbian, gay, bisexual and transgendered soldiers reported good working relationships with their peers; incidences of sexual harassment among women dropped; and not a single assault could be attributed to gay-bashing.

The study concluded that lifting the ban on openly gay members had no bearing on military performance, unit cohesion, or discipline.

He expects the same would be true if the U.S. dropped its 'Don't ask, don't tell' policy and says he's optimistic nay-sayers won't be able to stave off change for much longer.

"We know we're standing on the right side of history," he said.

| "Homosexuals still encounter consider-
able discrimination in [German mili-
tary] companies."

Germany Allows Gays in the Military, but They Still Face Discrimination

Brigitte Moll

Brigitte Moll is a writer and journalist. In the following view-point, she reports on a German soldier, Udo Kappler, who came out as gay. She says he was subsequently given poor performance evaluations and accused of harassing fellow soldiers. Moll notes that despite official policy that makes discrimination illegal, prejudice against gays remains a strong force in the German military, and many soldiers fear to tell their peers about their sexual orientation.

As you read, consider the following questions:

1. Before 1990, what reasons were given for preventing gays from serving in the German military, according to Moll?

2. What is the "Sexualerlass," as related by the author?

3. Who is Peer Uhlmann, and how does Moll say he has tried to change attitudes toward gays in the military?

In 1990, official discrimination against homosexuality in the Bundeswehr—the German military—was lifted, with gay men no longer being branded "emotionally vulnerable," and thus "compromising" to military engagements.

Discrimination and False Accusations

Udo Kappler, however, can tell you that the reality is different. His story is proof that homosexuals still encounter considerable discrimination in Bundeswehr companies.

Until two years ago [in 2007], Udo Kappler was just another paratrooper in his division near Oldenburg in the northwest of Germany. He kept a low profile, as soldiers do. That is, until the then 42-year-old came out and exposed his sexuality to the world—and his fellow soldiers.

"After I came out of the closet, I was told almost immediately in writing that my performance was lacking," Kappler told *Deutsche Welle*.

"However, the funny thing is that they didn't tell me why or justify it like they normally do in such cases. From one day to the next, I was all of a sudden the 'worst soldier' in my company."

Indeed, before exposing his homosexuality, the professional paratrooper belonged to the top 20 percent of his division. Almost immediately thereafter, Kappler found himself at the bottom of the performance ranking.

Kappler decided to defend himself. He brought his case to the Bundeswehr's equal opportunity commissioner, with initial success. His superiors repealed their evaluation.

However, after a fleeting return to normalcy, the situation then became surreal. Out of the blue, a group of Kappler's fellow soldiers accused their gay colleague of sexual assault—against another male soldier.

Homophobia in Germany

A hotline for victims of gay hate crime ... recently released results of a new poll that suggest an increase in homophobic crime in Germany....

40.6 percent of the 17,500 men who responded to the Germany-wide online poll say they suffered hate crimes in 2007. The crimes include anything illegal under German law, from verbal insults and spitting to serious assault. But the number is up from 35.5 percent in 2006.

Michael Scott Moore, Der Spiegel, *July 3, 2008.*

Kappler turned to a Bundeswehr legal advisor, who began an investigation and questioned all those involved in the case—including Kappler.

Encouraging Discrimination

"After the legal advisor started the investigation, it became clear that the allegations had been completely made up. The so-called witnesses were forced by their superiors to incriminate me. But when I was questioned, even the legal advisor was asking questions that had nothing to do with my role in the military. It was too private," Kappler said.

The legal advisor decided in favor of Kappler, in accordance with the Bundeswehr's "Sexualerlass," or sexual decree, which forbids the discrimination [against] gay soldiers.

The Bundeswehr responded to the sexual allegations with a statement:

"The German military demands that superior officers establish and enforce an atmosphere of tolerance with regard to sexual orientation among soldiers. The German military can't exclude infringements of non-discrimination laws; these infringements, however, will not be tolerated."

As Kappler's case shows, though, the reality is that discrimination is not just tolerated by some superior officers: in certain cases it is even encouraged.

Some say Kappler's case exposes just the tip of the iceberg when it comes to anti-homosexual tendencies in the German military. Bundeswehr soldiers who have already come out with their homosexuality, meanwhile, are taking steps to help other gay soldiers do the same.

Peer Uhlmann, a 29-year-old openly gay Bundeswehr captain heads a working group reaching out to gays in the Germany military.

"The topic of homosexuality is totally repressed in the Bundeswehr. Sure, there's this 'Sexualerlass,' which technically allows gays to be soldiers and to be open about their sexuality, but that hasn't changed anything," Uhlmann said.

Superior officers in particular, according to Uhlmann, are the ones that should be fighting against discrimination. Only this way, he says, will soldiers trust themselves to be open about their sexuality.

For the most part, as was seen in the case of Udo Kappler, homosexuality remains a taboo within German troop divisions. In his opinion, the average soldier's view of homosexuality is dominated by stereotypes.

"Around here gay soldiers are viewed as wimps or as feminine," Kappler said. "It's a big problem for men anywhere to be labeled 'effeminate,' especially in the military. On the one side there is the heterosexual soldier with his big gun—and then there's the gay soldier with his pink hand bag."

Yet to this day, Kappler remains part of the Bundeswehr. He is no longer a paratrooper, having decided to take on an office job instead in a different division. He says he lives a happy life with his partner and enjoys not having to hide who he is.

But after the legal mess he was made to go through, Kappler is still waiting for one thing: a new, amended evaluation of his performance while a soldier in the German military.

Periodical and Internet Sources Bibliography

The following articles have been selected to supplement the diverse views presented in this chapter.

Aaron Belkin	"Study Finds Gays Do Not Undermine Canadian Military Performance," Palm Center, April 18, 2000. www.palmcenter.org.
Aaron Belkin and Jason McNichol	"The Effects of Including Gay and Lesbian Soldiers in the Australian Defense Forces: Appraising the Evidence," Palm Center, September 1, 2000. www.palmcenter.org.
Yermi Brenner	"Gays in the Israeli Military," *Huffington Post*, June 8, 2010. www.huffingtonpost.com.
Nathaniel Frank	"Russia Joins U.S. and Turkey in Barring Gays from Military Service," Palm Center, March 17, 2003. www.palmcenter.org.
Pauline Jelinek	"John Sheehan, Retired US General, Links Gays in Military to Genocide in Bosnia," *Huffington Post*, March 18, 2010. www.huffingtonpost.com.
Danny Kaplan	"Foreign Policy: Learning from Israel's Gays in Service," National Public Radio, May 26, 2010. www.npr.org.
Sarah Lyall	"Despite Misgivings, Gays Blend into British Military," *New York Times*, May 16, 2007. www.nytimes.com.
Sarah Lyall	"Gay Britons Serve in Military with Little Fuss, as Predicted Discord Does Not Occur," *New York Times*, May 21, 2007. www.nytimes.com.
Kayla Webley	"Brief History of Gays in the Military," *Time*, February 2, 2010. www.time.com.

For Further Discussion

Chapter 1

1. Based on the viewpoint by Anonymous, what would be the results of a national vote or referendum on allowing gays in the military? Would Cal Thomas support such a vote? Why or why not, and do you think Thomas's reasoning is sound?

Chapter 2

1. What policy does it seem like Thornberry and Sprigg would prefer to DADT? Based on the discussions in the viewpoints in Chapter 1, would such a change in policy have popular support?

Chapter 3

1. David A. Noebel argues that the military may impose a quota requiring that 10 percent of officers be homosexuals. Does Barack Obama propose this in his speech? Do any other authors in the book suggest that such a quota is likely? On what basis does Noebel argue that such a quota may be put in place, and is this a convincing argument? Why or why not?

2. DADT repeal was passed by the House in May 2010 and by the Senate Armed Services Committee in the same month, making repeal likely before the end of Obama's first term. Given this, does Matthew Yglesias's viewpoint seem justified? Does Jay Bookman's? Explain your answer.

Chapter 4

1. According to Brigitte Moll, what problems has Germany had in integrating gay soldiers into the military? Based on

other viewpoints in this chapter, do other nations seem to have had similar problems? Do you think the United States would have similar problems? Why or why not?

Organizations to Contact

The editors have compiled the following list of organizations concerned with the issues debated in this book. The descriptions are derived from materials provided by the organizations. All have publications or information available for interested readers. The list was compiled on the date of publication of the present volume; the information provided here may change. Be aware that many organizations take several weeks or longer to respond to inquiries, so allow as much time as possible.

American Civil Liberties Union (ACLU)
125 Broad St., 18th Fl., New York, NY   10004-2400
(212) 549-2500
e-mail: aclu@aclu.org
website: www.aclu.org

The ACLU is a national organization that champions American civil rights. The union maintains the position that government expediency and national security should not compromise fundamental civil liberties. It publishes and distributes policy statements, pamphlets, and press releases, including "Military Leaders Testify in Favor of Ending Discriminatory 'Don't Ask, Don't Tell' Policy," and "Military Wife Speaks Out on DADT Repeal—'Good Riddance.'"

Canadian Department of National Defense
101 Colonel By Dr.
Ottawa, ON   K1A 0K2 Canada
(613) 995-2534 • fax: (613) 992-4739
website: www.forces.gc.ca

The Canadian Department of National Defense is the department within the government of Canada responsible for all matters concerning the defense of Canada. It includes the Canadian military, known as the Canadian forces, as well as civilian personnel. Is Web site includes the weekly publication the *Maple Leaf*, the *Canada First* defense strategy blueprint, and numerous other articles and items, including "The Social Evolution of the Canadian Forces—post Somalia."

Center for Military Readiness (CMR)

PO Box 51600, Livonia, MI   48151
(202) 347-5333
e-mail: info@cmrlink.org
website: www.cmrlink.org

The Center for Military Readiness is an independent, nonpartisan educational organization formed to take a leadership role in promoting sound military personnel policies in the armed forces. Among its issues, CMR advocates strict enforcement of the law banning open homosexuality in the military. The organization publishes a magazine, *CMR Notes*, ten times a year, as well as periodic reports. Its website collects news articles and opinion pieces about homosexuals in the military dating back to 2001.

Family Research Institute (FRI)

PO Box 62640, Colorado Springs, CO   80962-2640
(303) 681-3113
website: www.familyresearchinst.org

Family Research Institute, a nonprofit scientific and educational corporation, works to preserve what it sees as America's historic moral framework and the traditional family. FRI produces scientific data on pressing social issues—especially homosexuality—in an effort to promote traditional policies. The group publishes a monthly newsletter, *Family Research Report*, back issues of which are available online. Its website also provides special reports, published articles, and pamphlets on the causes and effects of homosexuality.

Human Rights Campaign (HRC)

1640 Rhode Island Ave. NW, Washington, DC   20036-3278
(800) 777-4723 • fax: (202) 347-5323

e-mail: hrc@hrc.org
website: http://hrc.org

The Human Rights Campaign is America's largest civil rights organization working to achieve gay, lesbian, bisexual, and transgender (GLBT) equality. By engaging all Americans, HRC strives to end discrimination against GLBT citizens and realize a nation that achieves fundamental fairness and equality for all. HRC publishes *Equality*, which covers a range of topics that affect GLBT Americans.

Michael D. Palm Center

University of California, Santa Barbara, CA   93106-9420
(805) 893-5664
website: www.palmcenter.org

The Michael D. Palm Center is a research institute at the University of California–Santa Barbara that sponsors state-of-the-art research about critical and controversial issues. The center's priority, the "Don't Ask, Don't Tell" Project, continues the work of the former Center for the Study of Sexual Minorities in the Military in researching the integration of gays and lesbians into the military. The center publishes an online monthly newsletter, available through e-mail subscription, as well as press releases and reports such as "Presence of Openly Gay Soldiers in IDF Does Not Undermine Unit Social Cohesion," and "What Does the Empirical Research Say About the Impact of Openly Gay Service on the Military?"

Reason Foundation

3415 S. Sepulveda Blvd., Ste. 400, Los Angeles, CA   90034
(310) 391-2245 • fax: (310) 391-4395
website: www.reason.org

The foundation promotes individual freedoms and free-market principles, and opposes U.S. interventionism in foreign affairs. Its publications include the monthly *Reason* magazine, recent issues of which are available at www.reason.com. The foundation website, linked to the Reason Public Policy Institute, publishes online versions of institute articles and reports, such as "Obama's Betrayal on Don't Ask Don't Tell," and "Time to Replace Don't Ask, Don't Tell with When Asked, Do Tell."

Servicemembers Legal Defense Network (SLDN)

PO Box 65301, Washington, DC   20035-5301
(202) 328-3244 • fax: (202) 797-1635
e-mail: sldn@sldn.org
website: www.sldn.org

SLDN is a national nonprofit legal services, watchdog, and policy organization dedicated to ending discrimination against and harassment of military personnel affected by the "Don't Ask, Don't Tell" law banning military service by lesbian, gay, and bisexual persons and related forms of intolerance. It provides free legal counseling to service members with legal issues stemming from or related to the "Don't Ask, Don't Tell" law, the regulations governing military service by HIV-positive people, and the regulations addressing military service by transgender persons. SLDN publishes the *Survival Guide*, the most comprehensive resource available for service members, their families, and friends regarding "Don't Ask, Don't Tell" and related forms of discrimination. Its website also includes "Stories from the Frontlines: Letters to President Barack Obama," in which service members discuss their experiences with "Don't Ask, Don't Tell."

Servicemembers United

Washington, DC
(202) 349-1125
e-mail: info@servicemembersunited.org
website: http://servicemembersunited.org

Servicemembers United is a nonpartisan and nonprofit organization whose primary goals are to engage in education and advocacy on issues affecting gay and lesbian troops and veterans; to serve as an associational organization for the gay and lesbian military, veteran, and defense community; to represent the voice of Iraq/Afghanistan-era gay and lesbian troops and veterans; and to forward and inform public debate on the U.S. military's "Don't Ask, Don't Tell" policy. Its website includes a DADT digital archive with a large collection of materials relating to the "Don't Ask, Don't Tell" policy, as well as blogs, links, and press releases.

U.S. Department of Defense

Office of Public Communication,
Assistant Secretary of Defense for Public Affairs,
Washington, DC 20310-1400
(703) 428-0711
website: www.defenselink.mil

The U.S. Department of Defense is the agency within the U.S. government charged with providing armed protection for the country as a whole. The department includes all branches of the military and provides a central organizing body for them. The department's website offers numerous publications and presentations relating to national security and justification for actions taken by the military.

Bibliography of Books

Aaron Belkin and Geoffrey Bateman, eds.
Don't Ask, Don't Tell: Debating the Gay Ban in the Military. Boulder, CO: Lynne Rienner, 2003.

Allan Berube
Coming Out Under Fire: The History of Gay Men and Women in World War Two. New York: Free Press, 1990.

Kingsley Browne
Co-ed Combat: The New Evidence That Women Shouldn't Fight the Nation's Wars. New York: Penguin, 2007.

B. Burg
Gay Warriors: A Documentary History from the Ancient World to the Present. New York: New York University Press, 2002.

Margot Canaday
The Straight State: Sexuality and Citizenship in Twentieth-Century America. Princeton, NJ: Princeton University Press, 2009.

Melissa Sheridan Embser-Herbert
The U.S. Military's Don't Ask, Don't Tell Policy: A Reference Handbook. Westport, CT: Greenwood, 2007.

Steve Estes
Ask & Tell: Gay and Lesbian Veterans Speak Out. Chapel Hill: University of North Carolina Press, 2007.

Nathaniel Frank
Unfriendly Fire: How the Gay Ban Undermines the Military and Weakens America. New York: St. Martin's Press, 2009.

Zsa Zsa Gershick   *Secret Service: Untold Stories of Lesbians in the Military*. New York: Alyson Books, 2005.

Janet Halley   *Don't: A Reader's Guide to the Military's Anti-gay Policy*. Durham, NC: Duke University Press, 1999.

Melissa S. Herbert   *Camouflage Isn't Only for Combat: Gender, Sexuality, and Women in the Military*. New York: New York University Press, 2000.

Gregory M. Herek, Jared B. Jobe, and Ralph M. Carney, eds.   *Out in Force: Sexual Orientation and the Military*. Chicago: University of Chicago Press, 1996.

Kristin Holmstedt   *Band of Sisters: American Women at War in Iraq*. Mechanicsburg, PA: Stackpole Books, 2007.

Mary Ann Humphrey   *My Country, My Right to Serve: Experiences of Gay Men and Women in the Military, World War II to the Present*. New York: HarperPerennial, 1991.

Mic Hunter   *Honor Betrayed: Sexual Abuse in America's Military*. Fort Lee, NJ: Barricade Books, 2007.

Paul Jackson   *One of the Boys: Homosexuality in the Military During World War II*. Montreal: McGill-Queens University Press, 2010.

Gary L. Lehring   *Officially Gay: The Political Construction of Sexuality by the U.S. Military.* Philadelphia: Temple University Press, 2003.

Jeffrey McGowan   *Major Conflict: One Gay Man's Life in the Don't-Ask-Don't-Tell Military.* New York: Broadway Books, 2005.

Gary Mucciaroni   *Same Sex, Different Politics: Success and Failure in the Struggles over Gay Rights.* Chicago: University of Chicago Press, 2008.

Terri Spahr Nelson   *For Love of Country: Confronting Rape and Sexual Harassment in the U.S. Military.* Binghamton, NY: Haworth Press, 2002.

David A.J. Richards   *The Case for Gay Rights: From* Bowers *to* Lawrence *and Beyond.* Lawrence: University Press of Kansas, 2005.

Alan Sears and Craig Osten   *The Homosexual Agenda: Exposing the Principal Threat to Religious Freedom.* Nashville: Broadman & Holman, 2003.

Randy Shilts   *Conduct Unbecoming: Gays and Lesbians in the U.S. Military.* New York: St. Martin's Press, 1994.

Erin Solaro   *Women in the Line of Fire: What You Should Know About Women in the Military.* Emeryville, CA: Seal Press, 2006.

Marc Wolinsky and Kenneth Sherrill, eds.	*Gays and the Military: Joseph Steffan versus the United States.* Princeton, NJ: Princeton University Press, 1993.

Index